Let's Get Infografit

We sit at computers all day (nights, too, on deadline), and as we age, our bodies begin to get rusty. Physical, mental, and nutritional health are all affected. Here's what to do about it—and how to explain it visually. The book does have a quick and easy exercise program, but it's also a how-to-show-it graphics manual with examples from Greek vases through 19th- and 20th-century exercise plans, as well as diagrams that explain how to prepare for other sports, and to repair any damage while participating in them. The book deals with many aspects of exercise: why it's good for you; what happens to your body if you don't move around enough; medical and anatomical explanations of soreness and exhaustion; the exhilaration of doing physical activity—the "runners' high." It also includes a chapter on nutrition. Driven by explanatory graphics—both historic and contemporary—*Let's Get Infografit*, is aimed at maintaining a level of fitness at all ages.

This is the tenth book that **Nigel Holmes** has written on information design and infographics. He is the former graphics director at *Time* magazine, has lectured globally, and has taught at Stanford and Yale. His diverse list of clients includes the BBC, Ford, Heinz, BMW, Sony, Estée Lauder, and Apple, and his work has appeared in a wide range of media including *The New York Times, Rolling Stone, Esquire, Sports Illustrated, New Scientist, National Geographic, Scientific American, and The New Yorker.* He has given three TED talks, his work has been exhibited internationally, and he is the recipient of multiple awards, including the Lifetime Achievement Award from the Society for News Design, and the Ladislav Sutnar Award.

Let's Get Infografit
A Graphic Look at Exercise and Health

Nigel Holmes

CRC Press
Taylor & Francis Group
Boca Raton London New York

CRC Press is an imprint of the
Taylor & Francis Group, an **informa** business

AN A K PETERS BOOK

Designed cover image: Nigel Holmes

First edition published 2026
by CRC Press
2385 NW Executive Center Drive, Suite 320, Boca Raton FL 33431

and by CRC Press
4 Park Square, Milton Park, Abingdon, Oxon, OX14 4RN

CRC Press is an imprint of Taylor & Francis Group, LLC

For Product Safety Concerns and Information please contact our EU representative:
GPSR@taylorandfrancis.com.
Taylor & Francis Verlag GmbH, Kaufingerstraße 24, 80331 München, Germany.

ISBN: 978-1-032-80404-0 (hbk)
ISBN: 978-1-032-77727-6 (pbk)
ISBN: 978-1-003-49671-7 (ebk)

DOI: 10.1201/ 9781003496717

Typeset in Gill Sans
by KnowledgeWorks Global Ltd

Mum in her
WWII
ambulance-
driver's uniform,
plus cigarette.
(1944)

This book is dedicated to two strong women:
my mother Hazel (↑), who kept me fit as a youngster,
by literally telling me to get back in the saddle when I
fell off a horse at her riding school.

And to my dear wife Erin (↓), who, some 60 years later,
persuaded me to join her at the gym, so that I would
remain a (somewhat) fit oldster.

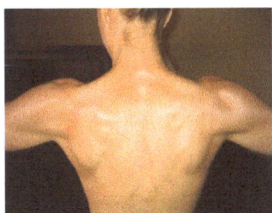

Erin is a bit
camera-shy, but
she did allow
me to show
her extremely
fit back! (2007)

Contents

Throughout the book narrow columns on the side of the pages will have asides (in blue, like this); most will have at least some tangential relevance to the text on the same page.

 However, this yellow imp means the blue aside might be slightly irrelevant. (But it might be fun.)

Meet

My expert collaborators

In the past, various critics have questioned my views about information graphics, perhaps because I was the "expert" when I wrote about the subject. Not this time. I needed help.

So, please meet three human experts who have put up with my odd requests, and my slow progress on this book. They'll be commenting on the text and the graphics, and adding their own ideas. (Blame them if you disagree!)

I asked **Phillip Kasofsky (Dr. K)** (→) to help me with medical topics. He's a long-time friend and the same age (old!), and he is currently in great demand as a fill-in emergency doctor in hospitals all over the Midwest. His career includes a wonderful mix of medicine and finance: he was the medical director for *Time* magazine (where we first met); a ghostwriter for countless medical papers; and a corporate executive, business consultant, diplomat, investment banker and money manager for more than 40 years.

Dr. Kasofsky was in the ER at Roosevelt Hospital on December 8, 1980, when a shooting victim was brought in. He realized it was John Lennon.

Phillip got undergraduate degrees from Columbia before getting his MD at NYU, then an MBA in Finance and Economics at the Stern School of Business. He was the first medical doctor to work in Wall Street, advising investors on new medical innovations— technologies such as artificial hearts, MRI scanners, pacemakers, gene machines, automatic electrical defibrillators, high–definition ultrasound, and medical lasers.

This book was inspired in part by Phillip's at-home exercise program, The Three-Rep, that has its own chapter, later on.

Next, for general fitness questions, I asked **Gene DeNota** (↓) for help. Gene is the Fitness Operations Coordinator at the YMCA in Darien, Connecticut. He has spent the last 30 years in the health and fitness industry helping people create healthy lifestyles.

Gene proposed to his wife Jill on the *Jumbotron* (giant TV) in front of 45,000 fans at a New York Yankees baseball game in July, 2011.

He and his two young sons (from a previous marriage) were celebrating a late Father's Day outing—at least that's the story they told Jill. They asked a friend to take a video of her reaction when the "Will you marry me?" message appeared on the big screen. The friend took the video, and Jill said yes. They have been married for 12 years.

He's worked as a fitness instructor, and personal trainer for many health clubs. He's also worked in the fitness equipment retail sales industry, setting up and installing home gyms.

Gene specializes in strength, cardio-vascular, and endurance training, as well as stretching to help increase flexibility. In addition, he is certified in sports nutrition. As well as one-on-one small group training, he teaches group classes which include kettlebells, extreme conditioning boot camps, and group weight training. Gene has a passion for the world of bodybuilding, and has participated in competitions.

Many other people offered suggestions—and graphics (see Chapter 8)—but there is one I must mention here. I first met **Marion Nestle** at a panel convened by The White House to discuss a graphic update to the government's dietary guidelines. The meeting—I was disappointed that it was not *at* The White House itself!—was during the Obama administration, and was part of Michelle Obama's *"Let's Move"* initiative.

You can see the results of the meeting on page 43.

Marion (←), dubbed an "obesity warrior" by *Time* magazine in 2004, and whose ideas are hugely influential in everything to do with nutrition, is the *Paulette Goddard Professor of Nutrition, Food Studies, and Public Health Emerita* at New York University. Her research

Yes, *that* Paulette Goddard, the movie star. She gave $20 million to NYU.

Marion's excellent (and almost daily) blog is foodpolitics.com

emphasizes the role of food marketing. She has written 15 books, including *Food Politics: How the Food Industry Influences Nutrition and Health*, 2002, and she was working on her 16th and 17th books when we met in her New York office in April 2024. Food writer Michael Pollan named Marion #2 on his list of *The World's 7 Most Powerful Foodies*, right after his #1 pick, Michelle Obama.

In *Forbes* magazine, 2011.

Her favorite food: ice cream. Marion kindly agreed to add some comments to my text.

Phillip told me he'd like to warn us to be wary of experts—not the three we have just met, of course! Take it away, Dr. K…

What are the basic elements of a successful "expert?"

The first element is a professional-looking appearance, style, manner, dress, vocabulary, assurance. TV doctors and many more have got it down pat. Some who started out with genuinely good intentions got caught up in success, money, and the need to keep presenting new things. Eventually they become less sound and less genuine, less scientific.

The second element is content. It must sound as if there is some scientific basis to what they are saying, and that it's applicable to an important aspect of your health.

The third is to make extreme claims while using a lot of "could, would should, might," words in the pitch.

For example, researchers recently reported in a leading scientific journal that the nervous impulse of brain cells varies in strength with the heartbeat. So, using this report, you could develop a false technical system claiming to increase people's heartbeats that could, would, should, affect their brain cells; exercise the brain more; get rid of metabolic junk; avoid dementia; improve mental training; diminish depression; raise IQ.

Call it *Brainersizers!* Or nerve cleansing! Spinal fluid detoxing! Neuronal strengthening! It doesn't matter that none of those great benefits were reported, or that the research was done in lab mice.

Remember what Einstein said: *Beware of expertise.* Use common sense, and read the small print (→).

So, are there any *real* experts?

Yes, but none are right all the time. They're just righter than the average person. It depends on the field. Doctors are often wrong. Economists are often really wrong. Investment advisors are often out-of-the-park wrong. Any field that has a wide range of divergent opinions often means they are *all* wrong.

It appears that Jenny Holzer agrees with Dr. K. (and Einstein). This (↓) is from her 2024 exhibition at the Guggenheim Museum, NY.

Buy now! New low price!

Actual small print on an internet video for a health supplement:
- *Results may vary*
- *Results may not be typical.*
- *Reviews or testimonials may be fictionalized.*

Originally created in 1989, Jenny Holzer's *Lightline, 2024* is an updated and augmented series of LED texts that swirl continuously around the five parapet walls that wind around and up the rotunda of Frank Lloyd Wright's classic 1959 Guggenheim building.

TWO

Intro

Two teenage journeys

At the end of one school year, I rode home on a bike. School was in Surrey, in the south of England. Home was in Yorkshire, in the north of England, 230 miles away. I was 16. (For about 35 miles of the journey, I got a lift from a lorry driver, somewhere in Lincolnshire.)

A year later, my mother, who ran a horse-riding school, thought it would be good publicity for her school if she staged a re-creation of Dick Turpin's last ride from Highgate, London, to York. On the way, he was captured at the Green Dragon pub, located right next to the riding school, in Welton, Yorkshire (where it still serves beer and food). I was to dress up as Turpin and recreate the ride on my horse, called *Judy*. The Automobile Association made us an off-the-main-roads map of the 180-mile trip. After some exhausting, hours-long training rides in Yorkshire, we decided that for the actual event I should ride for three hours, then rest (or sleep) for three hours; then ride for another three, and so on round the clock, day and night, for four days, so I would never get stiff. Animal rights activists got hold of the story and restricted us to 12 miles for each three-hour stint on the road—an easy four miles an hour for a horse. The activists had no need to worry: *Judy*, my plucky stand-in for Turpin's *Black Bess*, was fitter at the end of the ride than when we started.

So why am I telling you about these two trips?

At boarding school, I rode my bike a lot, fantasizing about the *Tour de France*. At home, I rode horses at my mother's school. Every time I switched from one to the other, my legs were painfully aware—for a few days—of the different muscles I used when riding a bike at school, then a horse at home. My legs had to get

Richard Turpin (real name, John Palmer) was a notorious highwayman in England. He was hanged in York on April 7th, 1739, for stealing horses.

We converted a 6-horse transporter into a space for *Judy*, and a sleeping area for myself, blacksmith Geoff Fox and driver Tony Sutton.

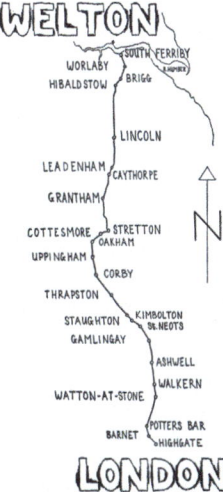

My first infographic—the Turpin ride—was published in *The Pony Club Book*, 1960.

used to a new experience, every time. In another chapter, I'll show you why my legs ached, and why different sports benefit from different warmups.

OK, let's get the elephant out of the room. I'm 83. Why on earth would anyone want to read a book about exercise from someone that old? Here are three answers—you may have others:

1. I'm still alive (and writing!).
2. You thought this was a book about infographics. (It is—kind of.)
3. You want to know how to stay fit, and you are happy to be here.

I like the idea expressed in the title of Toby Keith's song: *Don't Let The Old Man In*. As we age, it's easy to let "old" thoughts get in the way of other more constructive, optimistic, and creative ones *(see the Mindset graphic* →*)*. But along with our minds, we should also look after our bodies or they'll fail us—even if the spirit lives on. As an older person exercising in the gym with my 18-year-old granddaughter, it seemed that she sometimes had a harder time than I did, doing basic stretches. After my own teenage exploits on a bike and a horse, I wish I had started regular exercise as an adult earlier than I did—at age 63.

In the next chapters I'll show you some historical examples of exercise routines, and some simple things to do if you really don't have the time to go to a gym.

You've already met my collaborating experts: Dr. K will advise us on medical questions that relate to exercising and health, Gene will tell us how to get in shape for different sports, and Marion will help me explain metabolism and nutrition. There will also be illustrations of certain sports you might want to avoid.

There's always an elephant. In my last book, *Joyful Infographics*, it was an academic killjoy. Look it up on page 174. Or buy the book! (How many times have you seen a plug for the author's previous book on the second page of the new one?)

Toby Keith, the American country singer, was playing golf with Clint Eastwood, 88 at the time, and asked him, "How do you remain so young and active?" Clint's reply gave Toby a terrific song title.

Dr. K says:
I know a retired bull rider. He's alive, but looks pretty beat up, walks funny, and has broken every bone in his body…a few, several times.

Hmmm, perhaps we'll give this one a miss.

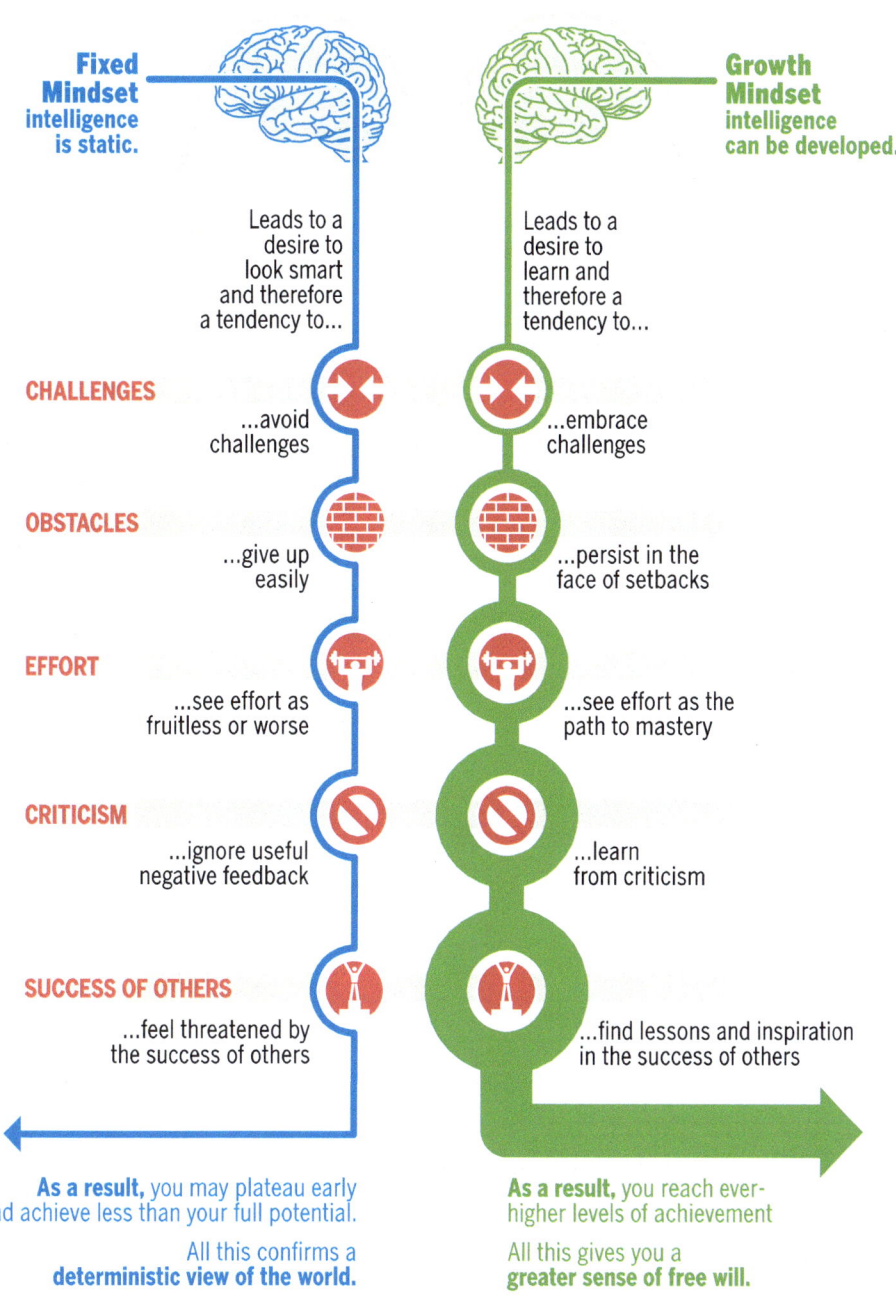

Fixed Mindset
intelligence is static.

Growth Mindset
intelligence can be developed.

Leads to a desire to look smart and therefore a tendency to...

Leads to a desire to learn and therefore a tendency to...

CHALLENGES
...avoid challenges

...embrace challenges

OBSTACLES
...give up easily

...persist in the face of setbacks

EFFORT
...see effort as fruitless or worse

...see effort as the path to mastery

CRITICISM
...ignore useful negative feedback

...learn from criticism

SUCCESS OF OTHERS
...feel threatened by the success of others

...find lessons and inspiration in the success of others

As a result, you may plateau early and achieve less than your full potential.
All this confirms a **deterministic view of the world.**

As a result, you reach ever-higher levels of achievement
All this gives you a **greater sense of free will.**

I made this diagram for *Stanford Magazine* in 2012 to go with an article about the work of Professor Carol Dweck. Although her theory of *Mindset* is usually applied to children and students, it's also clearly saying

Don't Let The Old Man In to everyone, and of any age. Elaine LaLanne (fitness guru Jack LaLanne's wife) had it right. She said—at age 97, in 2023— "Everything starts in the mind."

THREE
3

Past

"Let's start at the very beginning..." ♫

More about *The Sound of Music* a little later on.

Lots of books about the beginnings of infographics mention the 40,000-year-old paintings in French and Spanish caves as a sort of forerunner of modern graphics. But what about the history of *fitness* graphics?

Cave painters had to stay fit just to survive, but they hardly ever depicted themselves in *any* form, let alone doing any form of exercise. So this brief look at physical fitness in the past is going to move swiftly away from Europe, to the East.

Most people agree that the fitness industry we know today originated in **Ancient China and India,** around 4,500 years ago. In China, exercise—in the form of poses that were based on animal movements—was believed to prevent disease. In India, the practice of yoga was developed by the Hindu priest Maharishi Patanjali (↓), the "father of yoga," as a way to control and calm the mind. He wrote the texts known today as the *Yoga Sutras*.

The word **yoga** comes from the Sanskrit word *yuj,* meaning **union.**

Patanjali's eight principles of yoga:

1. *Yama* (restraint)
2. *Niyama* (discipline)
3. *Asana* (seat, or exercises—what most people think of as yoga today)
4. *Pranayama* (breath control)
5. *Pratyahara* (withdrawal of the senses from the outer world)
6. *Dharana* (concentration of the mind)
7. *Dhyana* (concentrated meditation)
8. *Samadhi* (total enlightenment)

On to **Greece** and the original Olympic Games, in 776 BC.

Ok, I'm skipping Assyrians, Egyptians, and others who prepared their youths for war by insisting on physical training. Apart from simply keeping their armies in fighting shape, that very training—for instance, javelin and discus throwing—is what some of the original Olympic sports were based on.

The word **Olympiad** was used in ancient Greece to mean a period of four years.

Married women could not take part or even watch the Olympics; Unmarried women were allowed to attend the competitions.

The Olympics aren't the oldest pictorial examples of people being sporty. Early Hittite bull-leaping is recorded on vases from about 1650 BC. But you'll be happy to know that we won't be discussing that sort of exercise, even though it does still happen in France, Spain, and India.

Here's a typical black-figure image of a marathon runner. It's from a Panathenaic prize amphora (↓), in the Metropolitan Museum of Art, New York, dated about 530 BC, and attributed to the Greek artist Euphiletos.

The vase was filled with 38 liters of olive oil when presented to winning competitors (as well as a crown of laurel leaves)..

The Greeks recorded a number of sports on painted vases, including this weight-assisted long-jumper (↓), from 540 BC. But while the names of the first Olympic athletes are well-known, statistics about their jumps and speeds are not, so we don't know whether this guy would beat Mike Powell's 8.95m (29ft 4.25in) leap 2,531 years later, in 1991—with or without weights. (Not to mention with or without clothes.)

In 520 BC, the Olympics included a new event: the hoplite race. Before it became an Olympic sport, such races were run in full 27kg (60lb) armor (hoplite). Olympic contestants were naked except for helmets and shin guards, and carrying shields.

Bigfoot, Littlefoot
1996 US Olympic athletes' shoe sizes.

size 5.5
Dominique Moceanu
(gymnastics)

size 22
Shaquille O'Neal
(basketball)

There are claims that an Indian physician, Susruta, was the first to prescribe exercise for health reasons, in 600 BC. However, the earliest printed book about physical fitness, the *Book of Bodily Exercise* by Cristóbal Méndez, published during the Renaissance in 1553, ignored Susruta's work, as did the 1569 book *De Arte Gymnastica* by the Italian physician Girolamo Mercuriale. Instead, both books relied on Greek and Roman ideas about the value and benefits of exercise.

Susruta of India, an Unrecognized Contributor to the History of Exercise Physiology by Charles M. Tipton, The Journal of Applied Physiology, Vol. 104, No. 6

The **Middle Ages** (roughly the 1,000 years from the 5th to the 15th century) was a Muddled Age of political and religious ideas in Europe. Christians and other religious groups thought that you should spend your life preparing for the afterlife; your earthly body was unimportant. Like some earlier times, physical fitness was not considered worth pursuing—Catholics actually called exercising a sin—unless you were a man being trained to be a soldier.

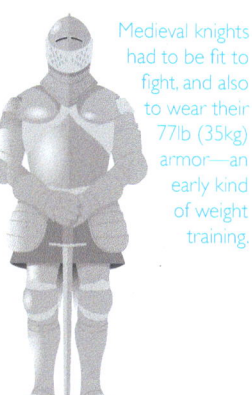

Medieval knights had to be fit to fight, and also to wear their 77lb (35kg) armor—an early kind of weight training.

The **Renaissance** changed that thinking.
During this period (roughly 1400–1600), along with the Méndez and Mercuriale books mentioned above, two artists in particular changed people's ideas about the body, by making spectacularly beautiful sculptures (Michelangelo), and amazing anatomical

studies (Leonardo). This began to shift popular perception away from the more spiritual and mental aspects of exercise towards an appreciation of aesthetics and an understanding of science.

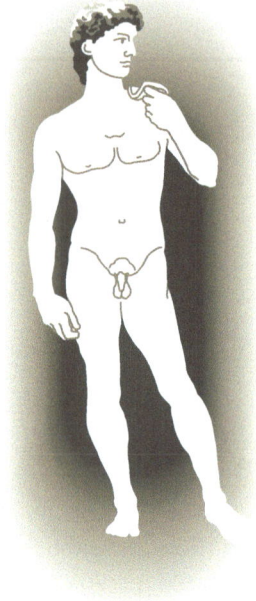

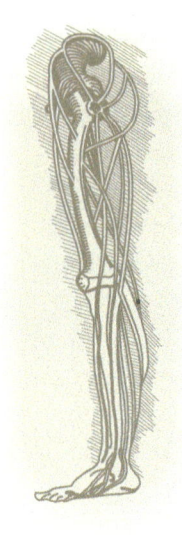

Michelangelo was 26 when he started work on *David*, in 1501. He finished the sculpture in 1504. (Avert your eyes if you are looking at this in Florida. But the book is probably banned there already.)

Leonardo drew the bones and tendons of the left leg in 1505. (And the *Mona Lisa?* He was painting her between 1503 and 1506.)

David by Michelangelo

*Leg by Leonardo
(odranoeL yb geL)*

Fitness as a business really took off in Europe during the **Industrial Revolution.** Gymnastics was the new thing, led by the German teacher Guts Muths, whose *Gymnastik für die Jugend* (1800) was a system of artistic movements, and it became *the* go-to fitness textbook. Another German teacher, Friedrich Jahn, emphasized the physical benefits of exercise and fitness over the more artistic side. Jahn created an open-air gymnasium in Berlin in 1811. Different forms of gymnastics were developed in Sweden, England, France, Spain, and Poland.

Muths was called the "Grandfather of Gymnastics."
Jahn was the "Father."
He invented the pommel horse and the parallel bars.

In the late **19th Century,** book production became cheaper, and fitness manuals with lots of pictures proliferated. *Theory and Practice of the Movement Cure,* by Charles F. Taylor, MD, recommends some slightly scary procedures, such as this "chest vibration with the springing board," (→).

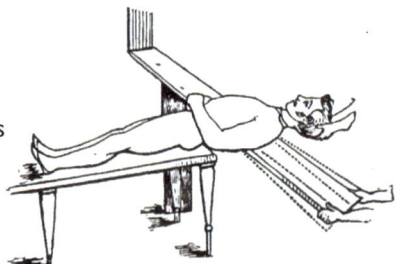

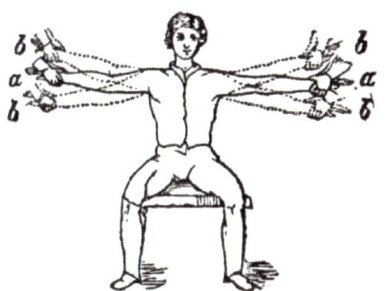

It was thought at that time that respiratory problems could be alleviated by being bounced around, or by having assistants stand on either side of the "patient," vigorously shaking his outstretched arms (←).

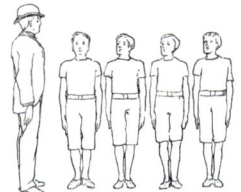

Donald Walker's *British Manly Exercises, from* 1834, includes nice sequential drawings of a rower:

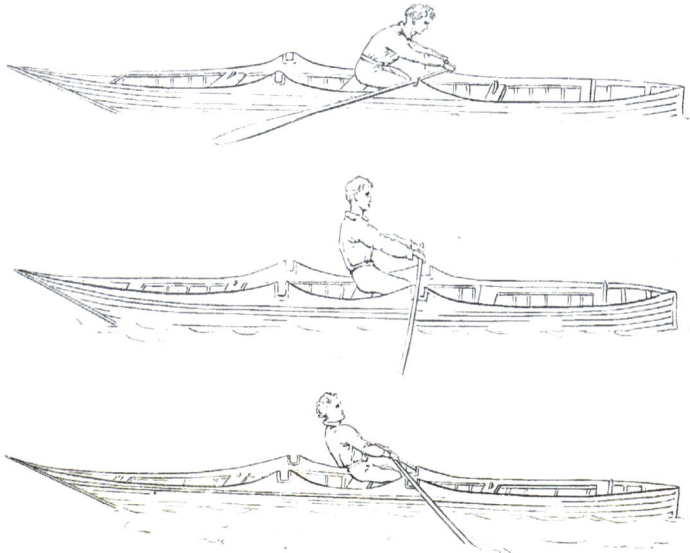

Walker's book has this proud announcement on the title page:
"British Manly Exercises, in which Rowing and sailing are now first described; and Riding and Driving are for the first time given in a work of this kind; as well as the usual subjects of Walking, Running, Leaping, Vaulting, Balancing, Scating (sic), Climbing, Swimming, Wrestling, Boxing, Training, &c. &c. &c."

And here's a finely drawn horse and rider, plus a gallant attempt to draw those notriously difficult parts of our anatomy—hands—showing various ways to hold the reins properly when riding:

Perhaps the most surprising book from this period is *The Portable Gym, A Manual of Exercises* by Gustav Ernst, published in 1864. It describes the forerunner of exercise machines seen in almost every gym today, although it's not exactly clear how or why it was thought to be *portable*. Here are five diagrams from the book, including what the author (or the uncredited artist) thought people would be wearing when they got going with their brand new contraption, at home.

The Age of the Bicycle

In 1817, Baron Karl von Drais invented the *laufmaschine* (running machine) which is generally credited as the first bicycle. In England and elsewhere, people called it a *velocipede* since it was propelled by the rider's feet. The original model was wooden, with iron rims on the wheels (↑).

In 1839, Kirkpatrick Macmillan made the first two-wheeled machine that was propelled by treadles attached with rods to a crank on the back wheel (→).

In 1860, Eugène Meyer invented the high-wheeler, putting the larger wheel in the front (←). Over the years, that wheel became even larger, making the bike more dangerous to ride—many wrists were broken trying to lessen the impact of toppling over the front when stopping. In England, it was known as the *Penny Farthing* (→), after the large penny and smaller farthing coins in use at the time.

In 1879, Harry Lawson invented the rear-chain-drive *Bicyclette* (←).

Finally, in 1885, John Kemp Starley invented the "safety bike," with equal-sized wheels (↓). Together with John Dunlop's tire, the modern bike was here, and it has stayed much the same for the next 140 years, (with lots of advances in materials, gears, brakes, shock absorbers and pedal-assist motors).

It didn't take long for Drais's wooden velocipede to be produced with metal parts, like the one above.

Full title: *L'Education Physique ou L'Entrainement Complet par la Methode Naturelle.*

The books are available today in facsimile, translated by Philippe Til.

The 20th Century. A big leap forward (pun intended) came in 1909 with the publication of Georges Hébert's *Natural Method,* three books of exercise instructions based on everyday activities—including jumping and balancing, as well as running and walking. Hébert was an officer in the French navy responsible for training the sailors.

There are a few drawings in his books, like this one demonstrating the right way to walk (→), but most illustrations are photos (↓ top). They mimic photographer Eadweard Muybridge's sequential photos in his book *The Human Figure in Motion,* 1885, (↓ bottom) which was an earlier revolution of its own.

Muybridge has been called the father of the motion picture. (Lots of "fathers of…" and "grandfathers of…" in this section. I suppose that can be expected in historical round-ups.)

Despite the women using the portable gym on the previous page, most physical fitness programs were designed for men. It was all about being manly (presumably to impress women).

Charles Atlas, "The World's Most Perfectly Developed Man," was the best known example of a fitness guru, after having sand kicked in his face when he was a skinny 97lb weakling. Atlas was born Angelo Siciliano in 1892. He changed his name in 1922, when he started the bodybuilding course *Dynamic Tension.* It was endorsed by famous athletes. Opposite, one of his comic-book print ads, that ran for years after his death at 80 in 1972.

Heavyweight champs Joe Louis (1930s and 40s), Rocky Marciano (50s), and Olympic gold medalist sprinter Allan Wells (Moscow 1980) all took the course.

At the school I went to, the activity we did in the gym was called physical jerks. I didn't realize then that George Orwell used these words in his 1949 novel *1984,* to describe the morning exercise routine that members of the Outer Party had to do in front of their telescreens, with instructions yapped at them by "a youngish woman, scrawny but muscular."

Recently I saw that *Physical Jerks* had been a BBC program years before, so readers would already have been familiar with the funny phrase when they read Orwell's book. This piece (←) is from the *Radio Times* dated November 24, 1939. Today, I still call what I do in the gym "physical jerks." It makes me smile. (By law in *1984,* Winston was *required* to smile at the screen. Big Brother was watching him.)

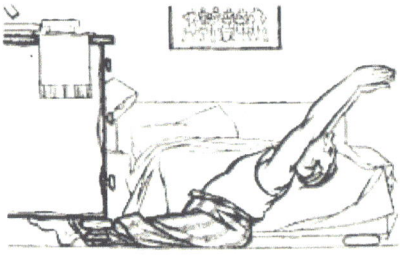

PHYSICAL JERKS

We are eagerly awaiting the beginning of the new early-morning broadcasts of physical jerks, which start on December 4 at 7.35 a.m. Whether or not we get out of bed and obey the voice of the loudspeaker, we shall at least enjoy feeling that the people who always liked doing physical jerks in the dawn are now able to do them in good company. On the Monday a male instructor will conduct exercises suitable for men. But even if the head of the household is driven reluctantly from his bed by female gibes, on the Tuesday he can blackmail his wife into doing the exercises for women, and so on. Thus both sexes will find themselves getting fitter and fitter, however unworthy their motives may be.

Some things will never change: editors at the BBC in 1939 assumed "the head of the household" was obviously a man.

I started to work for the *Radio Times* in 1970, and among a bunch of cuttings, I found several pages from 1957 that had lively drawings to help readers follow along with Eileen Fowler during her *Keep Fit* exercise programs. They were printed in pull-out supplements to save after you threw away the rest of the magazine's BBC's radio and TV schedules for the week. (More examples opposite, top.)

Lunge — and drop — and stretch—and back—and lunge — and flop

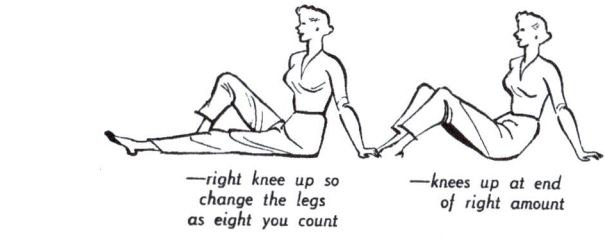

—right knee up so
change the legs
as eight you count

—knees up at end
of right amount

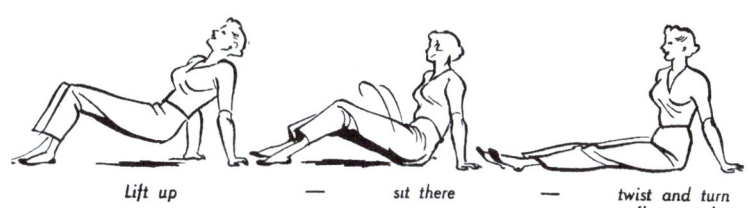

Lift up — sit there — twist and turn on floor or chair

My selective, short history of how fitness has been graphically explained is almost over, but we shouldn't forget a few influential presenters and teachers—such as Jack LaLanne's TV show (1951-85), and Jane Fonda's video aerobics, starting in 1982; her original *Workout* is the best selling video of all-time. Joseph Pilates (1883–1967) developed an exercise system (originally called *Contrology*) that had two parts—with and without machines—and was designed to strengthen the core. Pilates said, "I am not concerned with body building; I'm just trying to make people normal human beings." His most famous apparatus is the Reformer (↓).

See Jane Fonda on YouTube, and while you are there, catch Richard Simmons's (1948-2024) *Sweatin' to the Oldies* videos.

Users lie on a padded platform and push themselves back and forth along tracks, with different levels of resistance. Straps can be attached to hands and feet.

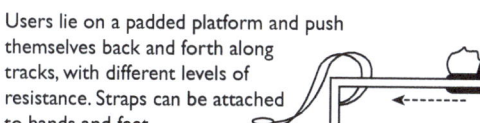

Look at Chapter 9, *Next*, for more future stuff, including Jane Fonda's move into virtual reality.

Finally, doesn't it seem that new ways to keep us fit are being sold to us nonstop? *Interactive training mirrors?*…very Orwellian!

On the other hand, not everyone wants to be in on the fitness craze. *Sketchers* advertises "Hands Free Slip-ins" which let you put your shoes on with "*NO* BENDING OVER. *NO* TOUCHING SHOES. *NO* KIDDING." In one of the ads, two young girls are wearing shoes they presumably haven't had to bend over to put on, and it includes this logo suggesting that even simple exercise is for suckers.

But please don't let that stop you from reading on!

NO MORE BENDING

4 FOUR

Body

Part 1. Anatomy: what's going on under our skin

Aaron Kuehn made these inspired typodiagrams.
As a designer, I'm jealous!

In part 1 of this chapter, you'll see other graphic
interpretations of bones and muscles and how they impact
our quest to get fit, but right now these are a
stylish way to start a chapter about
everything that goes on inside us,
including bones, muscles, and guts.

Part 2 of this chapter is about what
we put *into* our bodies: food and drugs;
but also diets, and nutrition in general.
(I'll also address the touchy subject of
weight and obesity.)

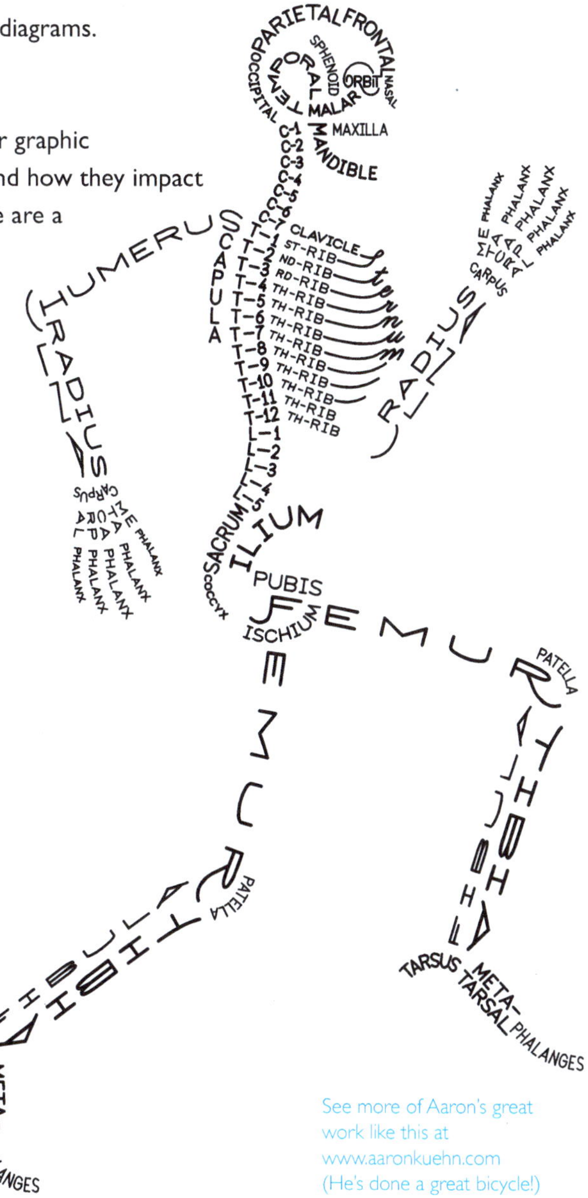

See more of Aaron's great
work like this at
www.aaronkuehn.com
(He's done a great bicycle!)

Musculature

i.e., muscles—I just can't resist a smashing four-syllable word that twists the tongue slightly. (I have included some tongue exercises in Chapter 10.)

There are about 650 voluntary, or skeletal, muscles in our bodies, over- and under-lapping each other. If I showed you them all, this simplified graphic would be completely covered with criss-crossing red lines, and you'd be confused. These are the major muscles we need to know. Don't be put off by the fancy Latin names!

Dr. K says:
Muscles almost always work in groups. Each group has another group that does the opposite, enabling both continuous motion and fine control.

The Sartorius muscle is sometimes called the tailor's muscle (*sartor* is the Latin word for tailor), because it made tailors' traditional cross-legged position more comfortable Hence *sartorial*—relating to tailored clothes.

Sources: *The American Medical Association Encyclopedia of Medicine; The Human Body,* Edited by Charles Clayman, MD; *Time Atlas of the Body; The World's Best Anatomical Charts;* Wikipedia

LEVATOR LABII SUPERIORIS
ZYGOMATICUS
RISORIUS
the three smile muscles—
should be exercised every day!

STERNOCLEIDOMASTOID
rotates your head and flexes your neck
(stiff neck? here's one of the problems)

TRAPEZIUS
draws your shoulders back and up
(lots more of this muscle on your back)

DELTOID
(delts)
raises your arms

PECTORALIS MAJOR
(pecs)
draws your arms forward
and inward

BICEPS
together with triceps, this bends
your arm at the elbow

SERRATUS ANTERIOR
draws shoulder blades forward;
helps when you push things

BRACHIORADIALIS
flexes your forearms
at the elbow

OBLIQUUS EXTERNUS
(abs)
squeezes your
abdominal area

SARTORIUS
bends your knees and thighs;
rotates thighs outwards

QUADRICEPS FEMORIS
(quads)
bend your thighs at hips; straighten knees

TIBIALIS ANTERIOR
draws your toes up; when standing,
this muscle keeps you vertical

SPLENIUS CAPITIS
when you say no, this is what's shaking your head
(also, it's another stiff neck culprit)

TRAPEZIUS
draws your shoulders back and up

DELTOID
(delts)
raises your arms

TRICEPS
+
BICEPS
working together, these two
raise and lower your arms

LATISSIMUS DORSI
(lats)
positioned under the Trapezius,
this muscle group stretches up to
the neck; it extends and rotates
your arms and shoulders

GLUTEUS MAXIMUS
(glutes)
extends your thighs when
walking and climbing

BICEPS FEMORIS
(hamstrings)
extends your thighs;
bends knees

GASTROCNEMIUS
(calves)
bends the knees when you walk;
extends feet when you jump

SOLEUS
maintains standing posture;
stops you from falling forward

ACHILLES TENDON
OK, not a muscle, but important!
The thickest tendon in your body,
connects the Gastrocnemius and
Soleus muscles to your heel bone.
It facilitates running and jumping

Gene says: If you'd like more
detail (much more) download
this great app: *imuscle2*

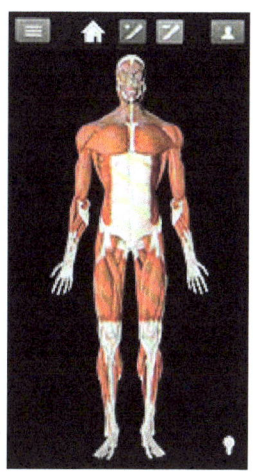

Achilles' Heel
When he was a baby, Achilles'
mum, Thetis, wanted him
to live forever, so she held
him by his heels and dipped
him head first into the River
Styx. But while most of him
would be protected by
this odd maneuver, his feet
didn't touch the water so
they would be the only part
of his body that would be
vulnerable to attack in the
future.

Achilles became a brave
fighting warrior. While
attempting to take Troy, a
poison dart was fired at his
vulnerable heel, and he died.

A Dutch anatomist, Philip
Verheyen, writing in 1693,
is credited with naming the
tendon the "cord of Achilles."

Muscles you use when you…

…run

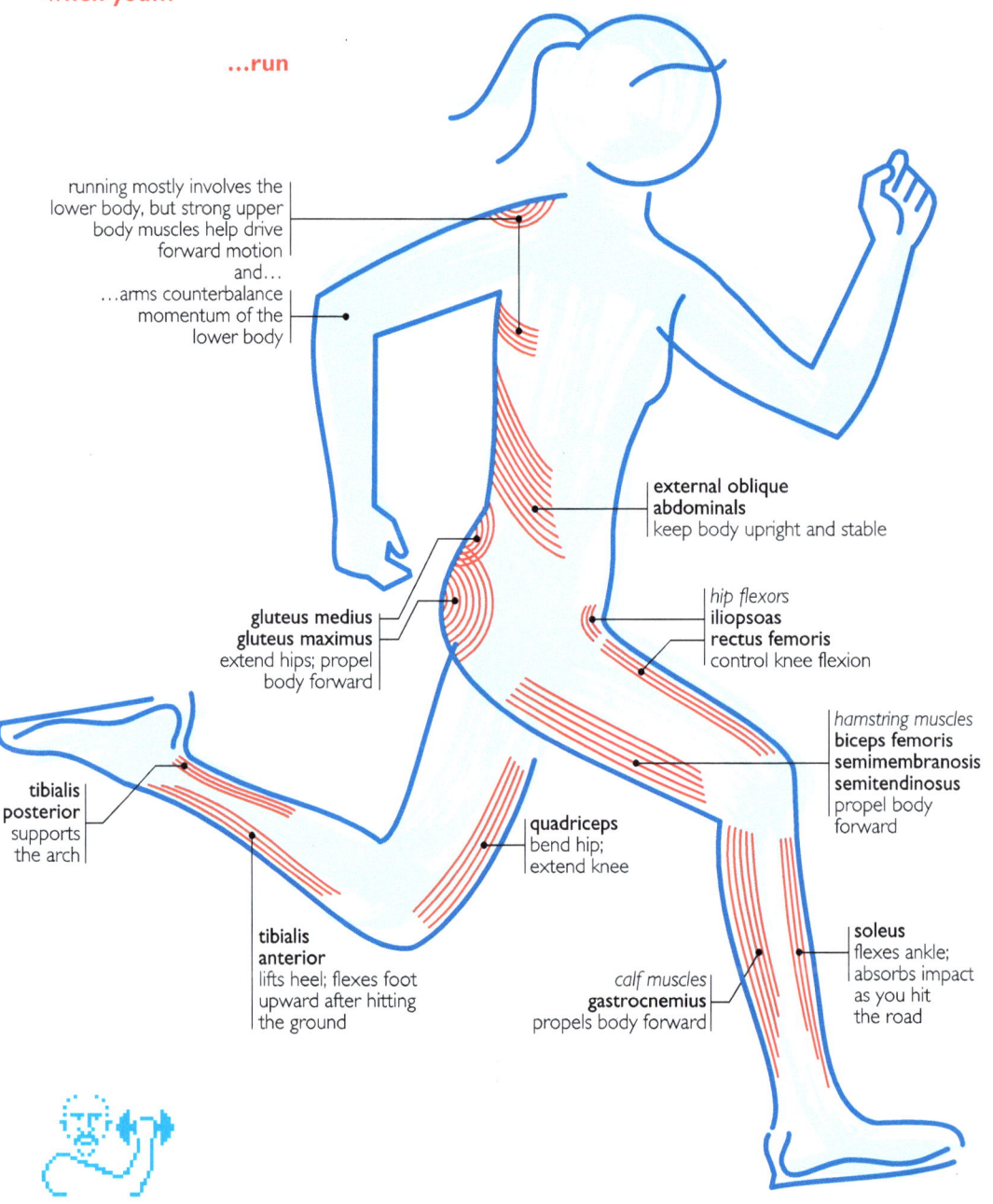

running mostly involves the lower body, but strong upper body muscles help drive forward motion and…

…arms counterbalance momentum of the lower body

external oblique abdominals keep body upright and stable

hip flexors **iliopsoas rectus femoris** control knee flexion

gluteus medius gluteus maximus extend hips; propel body forward

hamstring muscles **biceps femoris semimembranosis semitendinosus** propel body forward

tibialis posterior supports the arch

quadriceps bend hip; extend knee

tibialis anterior lifts heel; flexes foot upward after hitting the ground

calf muscles **gastrocnemius** propels body forward

soleus flexes ankle; absorbs impact as you hit the road

Gene says: I only run when I'm being chased! But running is a great full-body and cardio workout.

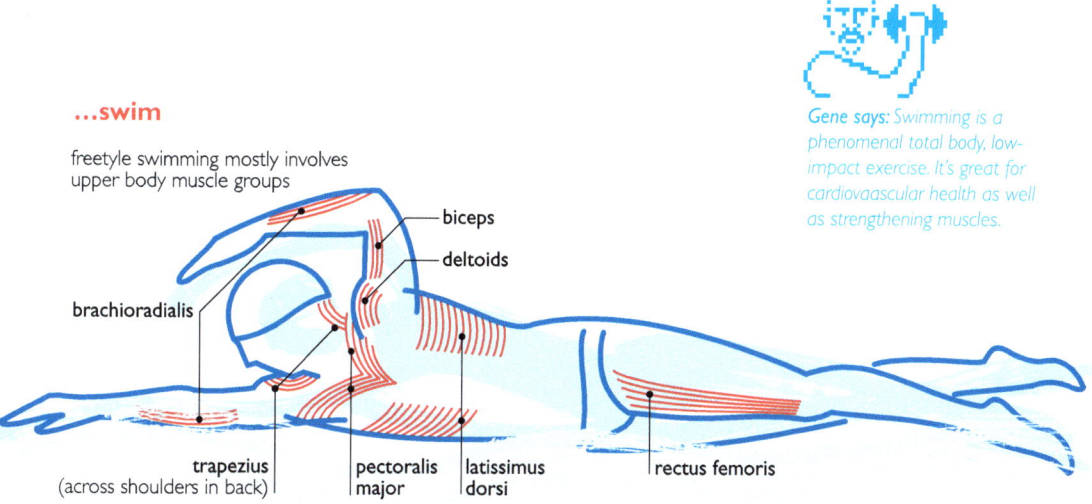

...swim

freetyle swimming mostly involves
upper body muscle groups

Gene says: Swimming is a
phenomenal total body, low-
impact exercise. It's great for
cardiovaascular health as well
as strengthening muscles.

biceps

deltoids

brachioradialis

trapezius
(across shoulders in back)

pectoralis
major

latissimus
dorsi

rectus femoris

...ski

Gene: When you ski, you are
primarily using your lower
body, and your core plays a
big part in stabilization.

gluteus medius
rotates thigh

gluteus maximus
rotates thigh and extends hip

quadriceps femoris

hamstring muscles
biceps femoris
semimembranosis
flex knee

adductor longus
flexes and rotates thigh

rectus femoris
vastus intermedius
extend knee

calf muscles
gastrocnemius

petronius longus
flexes foot

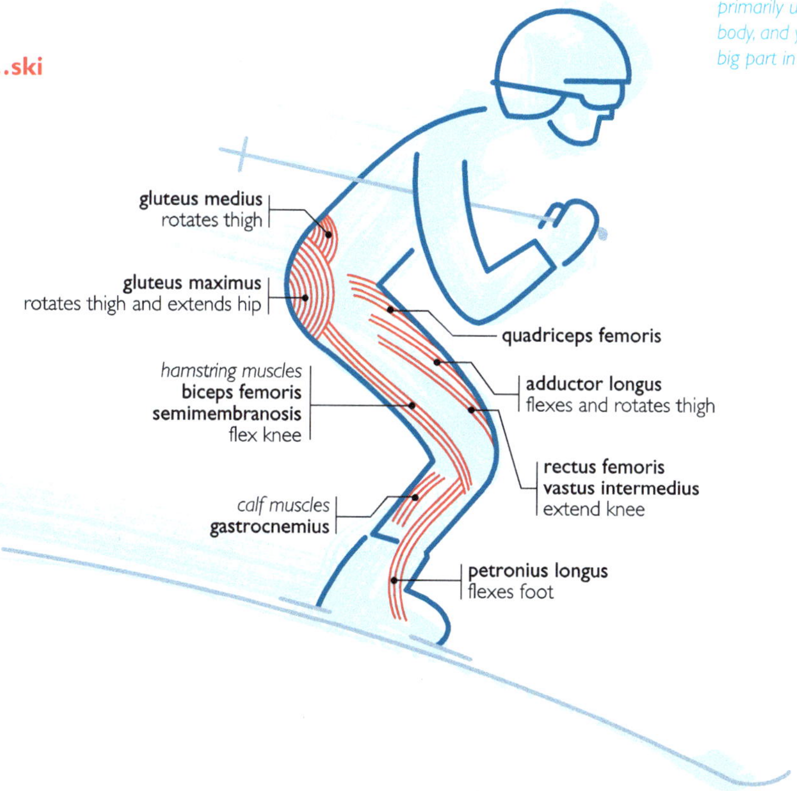

Muscles you use when you...

...ride a bike

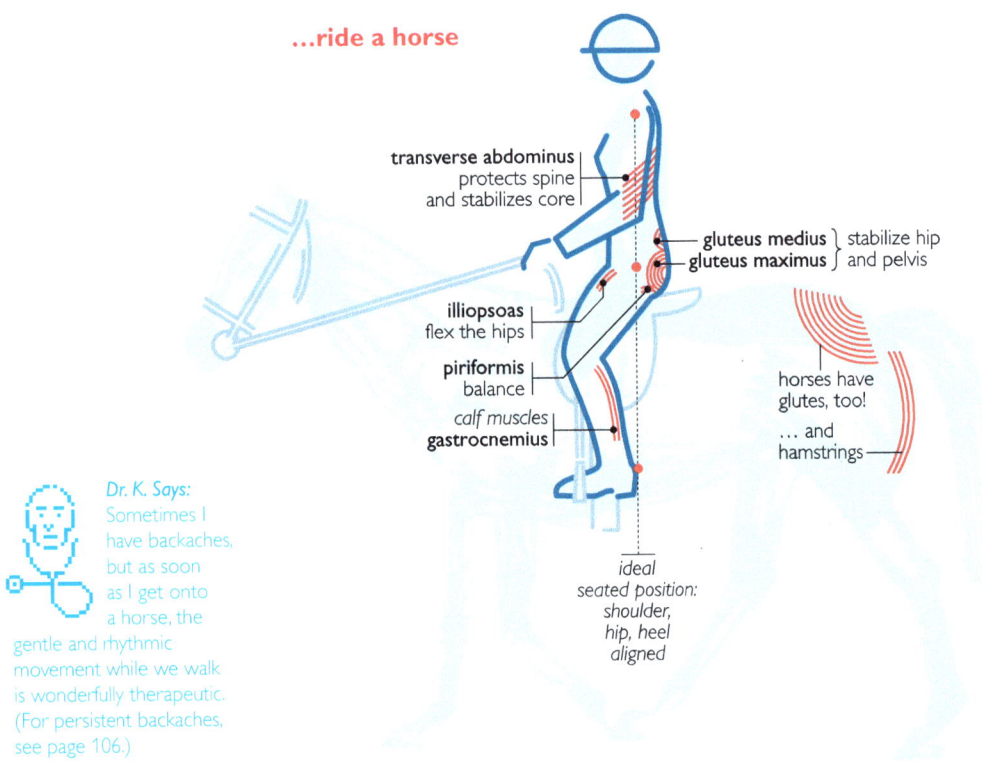

quads
rectus femoris
vastus intermedius
vastus lateralis

glutes
gluteus maximus

hamstring muscles
biceps femoris
semimembranosus

calf muscles
gastrocnemius

shin
tibialis anterior

soleus

Here's why my legs ached when I rode a bike for a while, then rode a horse. (See page 9.) Bike riders use leg muscles in relatively simple up-and-down movements. But when riding a horse, the legs are flexed in and out—both to stay balanced on your mount, and to send it commands.

...ride a horse

transverse abdominus
protects spine
and stabilizes core

gluteus medius } stabilize hip
gluteus maximus } and pelvis

illiopsoas
flex the hips

piriformis
balance

horses have
glutes, too!

... and
hamstrings

calf muscles
gastrocnemius

ideal
seated position:
shoulder,
hip, heel
aligned

Dr. K. Says:
Sometimes I have backaches, but as soon as I get onto a horse, the gentle and rhythmic movement while we walk is wonderfully therapeutic. (For persistent backaches, see page 106.)

...play golf

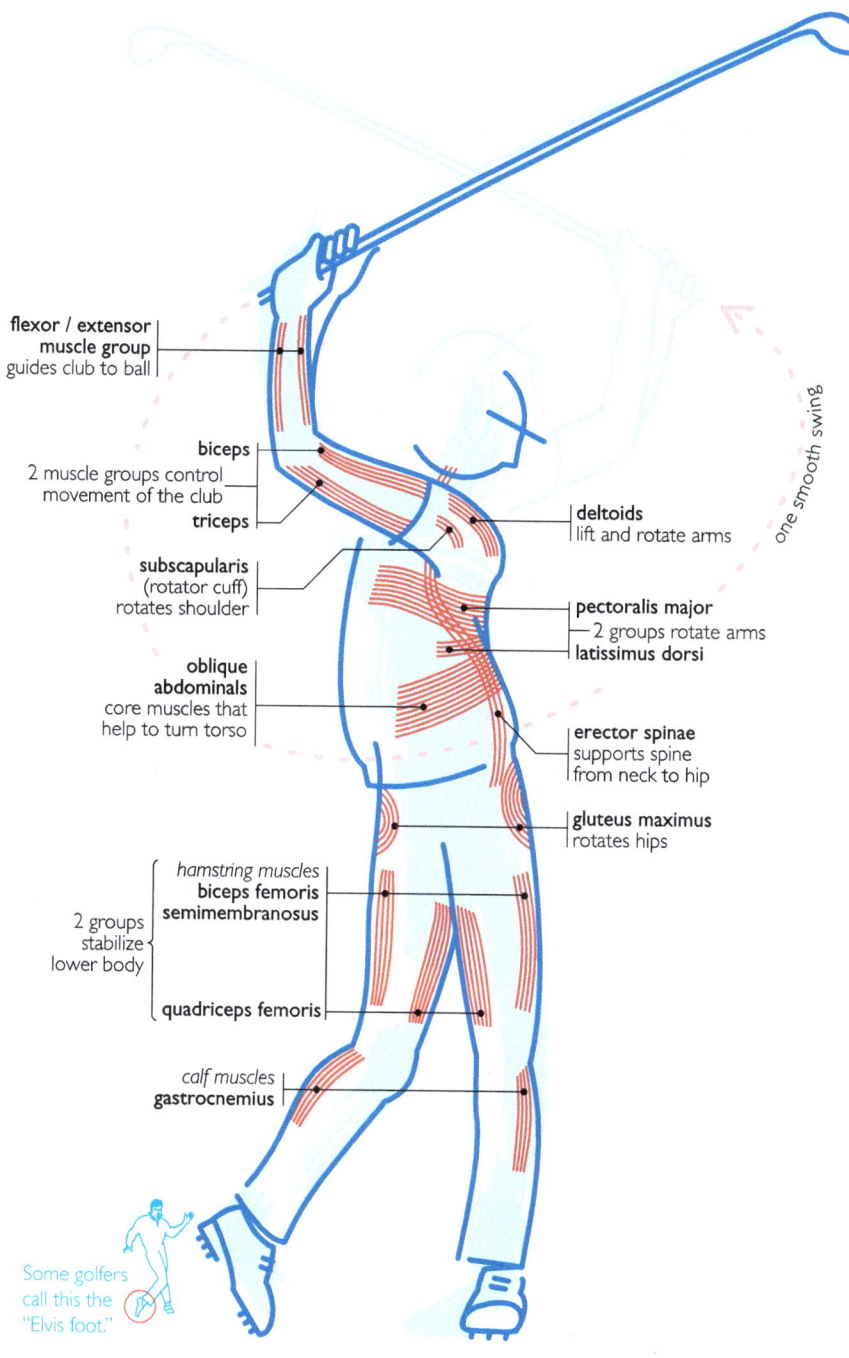

flexor / extensor
muscle group
guides club to ball

biceps
2 muscle groups control
movement of the club
triceps

subscapularis
(rotator cuff)
rotates shoulder

**oblique
abdominals**
core muscles that
help to turn torso

hamstring muscles
biceps femoris
semimembranosus

2 groups
stabilize
lower body

quadriceps femoris

calf muscles
gastrocnemius

deltoids
lift and rotate arms

pectoralis major
2 groups rotate arms
latissimus dorsi

erector spinae
supports spine
from neck to hip

gluteus maximus
rotates hips

one smooth swing

Some golfers
call this the
"Elvis foot."

Studies have found up to 500 obesity-related genes in humans. By themselves, genes don't *cause* obesity, but they can play a significant role.

Weight

A difficult subject. The problem might start with our *insides*, but if we have extra weight it's there for everyone to see on our *outsides*. Some of us inherited genes that predispose us to becoming heavier than the medical profession's—as well as fashion's—"ideal" weight. Others may just be eating too much.

Whatever the cause of those extra pounds or kilos might be, this is true: too much extra weight can result in health problems.

Here's how the book's resident doctor puts it:

Dr. K:

Why is the whole world increasingly overweight? Centuries ago, humans were not.

Three things happened:

1. Agriculture became big business, with commodity exchanges, international trade, gigantic farms—it became more and more productive with increasing yields.

2. Food itself became big business. Eating was encouraged for reasons other than hunger—it became a social activity, a treat, entertainment—and no longer a necessity for energy and nutrition. Mass production made food cheap, and companies added addictive ingredients to their products, (while making them less nutritious).

3. The Medical Industrial Complex stepped in with dietary products and pills to "solve" the problems. Increased profit became the driving force.

Result: we eat more food that is rich in weight-gaining ingredients, and this leads to weight-related problems—heart disease, high blood pressure, diabetes, arthritis, even some cancers.

So we turn to Big Pharma to cure us. But their weight-loss programs and diets often fail, looping us back to old eating habits.

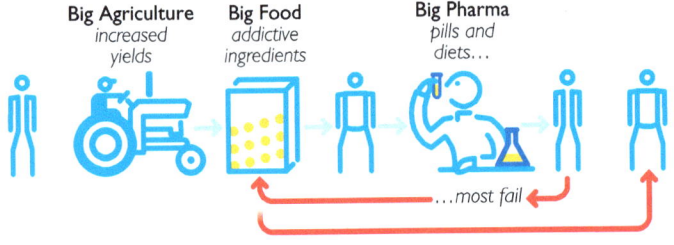

Big Agriculture
increased yields

Big Food
addictive ingredients

Big Pharma
pills and diets…

…most fail

Next pages: how biology shapes our bodies. First, metabolism (→).

METABOLISM: YOUR FOOD PROCESSOR

Metabolism encompasses a multitude of chemical changes in which **food** either builds and repairs cells, or is converted into energy.

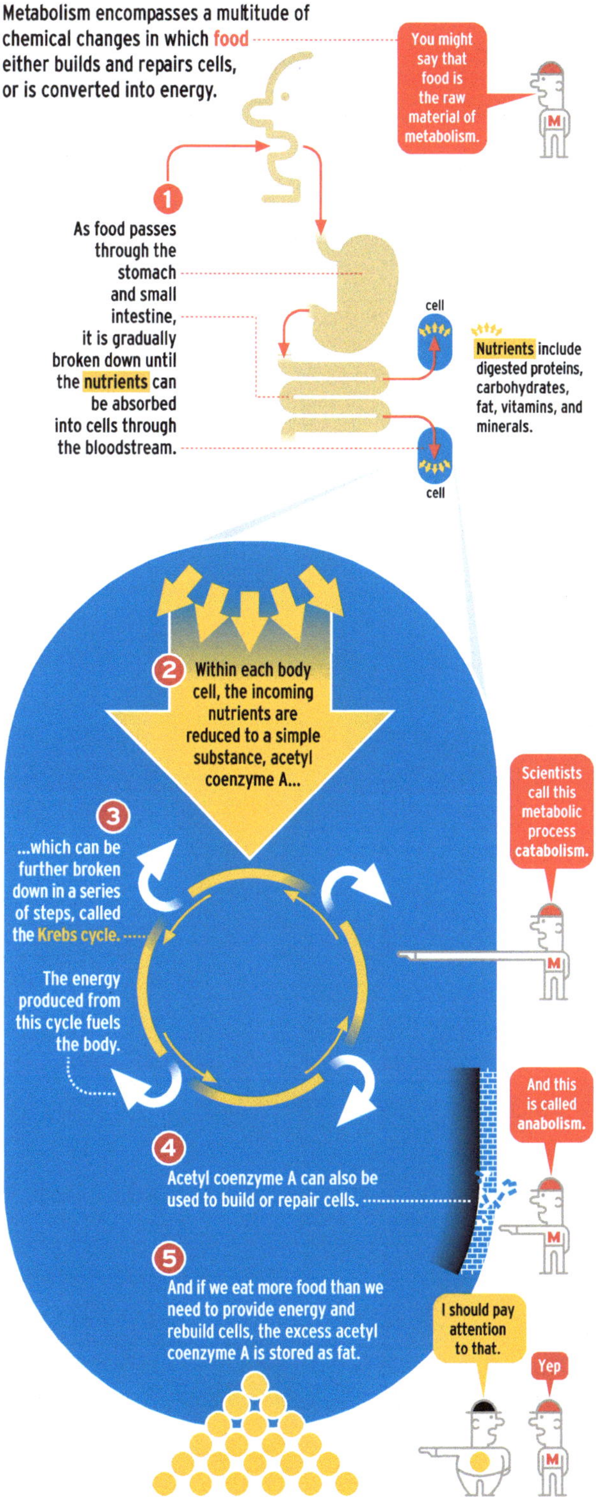

You might say that food is the raw material of metabolism.

1

As food passes through the stomach and small intestine, it is gradually broken down until the **nutrients** can be absorbed into cells through the bloodstream.

cell

Nutrients include digested proteins, carbohydrates, fat, vitamins, and minerals.

cell

2 Within each body cell, the incoming nutrients are reduced to a simple substance, acetyl coenzyme A...

Scientists call this metabolic process **catabolism**.

3

...which can be further broken down in a series of steps, called the **Krebs cycle**.

The energy produced from this cycle fuels the body.

And this is called **anabolism**.

4

Acetyl coenzyme A can also be used to build or repair cells.

5

And if we eat more food than we need to provide energy and rebuild cells, the excess acetyl coenzyme A is stored as fat.

I should pay attention to that.

Yep

Is there a genetic disposition to become obese?

Marion says: Genetics did not change in 1980 when people started eating more, so the real question is why did most people gain weight, while others did not? For most people, metabolism is set up to preserve glucose for the brain—its main source of energy—and therefore, body weight. Excess calories add up quickly if not used in physical activity. So the non-weight gainers are the exception. (They may be better educated and wealthier, and monitor what they eat.) Obesity is a matter of genetics, environment, plus metabolic factors (of which there are a great many).

 Really efficient metabolism

Pallas's long-tongued fruit bats consume their own weight in floral nectar—from an astounding 800 plants—during one night. Researchers in Northern Belize are studying how the *Glossophaga mutica* can eat so much sugar and not, to put it simply, die. That much sugar remaining in a human body would result in death. Perhaps there is a clue here that will lead science to help diabetes patients.

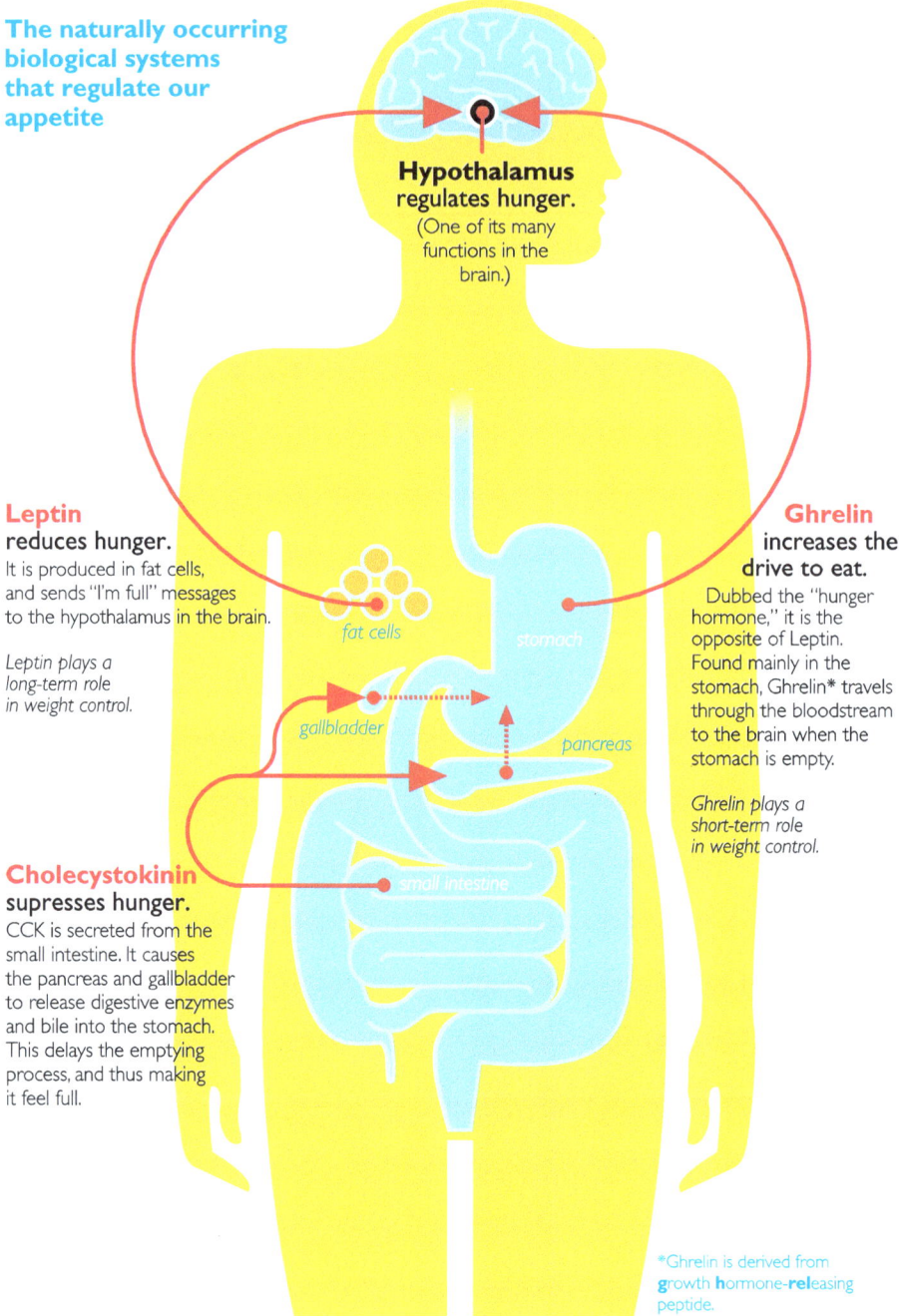

The naturally occurring biological systems that regulate our appetite

Hypothalamus regulates hunger.
(One of its many functions in the brain.)

Leptin reduces hunger.
It is produced in fat cells, and sends "I'm full" messages to the hypothalamus in the brain.

Leptin plays a long-term role in weight control.

fat cells

stomach

gallbladder

pancreas

Ghrelin increases the drive to eat.
Dubbed the "hunger hormone," it is the opposite of Leptin. Found mainly in the stomach, Ghrelin* travels through the bloodstream to the brain when the stomach is empty.

Ghrelin plays a short-term role in weight control.

Cholecystokinin supresses hunger.
CCK is secreted from the small intestine. It causes the pancreas and gallbladder to release digestive enzymes and bile into the stomach. This delays the emptying process, and thus making it feel full.

small intestine

*Ghrelin is derived from growth hormone-releasing peptide.

Leptin, cholecystokinin, and Ghrelin (↑) are three of the most important diet- and hunger-related hormones in our bodies. Others include GLP-1s (Glucagon-like Peptide-1s) which have led manufacturers such as Novo Nordisk and Eli Lilly to manufacture GLP-1RAs (Glucagon-like Peptide-1 Receptor Agonists). It's easy to be confused by pharma-scientific jargon, but I hope this diagram (→) helps.

What are GLP-1 Receptor Agonist medications?

Ozempic, Wegovy, Mounjaro, Zepbound are the best-known semaglutide medications that were originally developed to treat Type 2 Diabetes, and later found to result in weight loss for anyone, inluding diabetes patients, and there is evidence that semaglutides can be used to treat arthritis.

A great deal has been written (and sung →) about the drugs, especially in the wellness/fitness parts of the media—articles that emphasize the "it's not entirely your fault" arguments about obesity in general, and whether drugs are the ultimate answer to the worldwide obesity epidemic, especially when the price of the drugs can make them unaffordable for people whose insurance that doesn't cover them. In 2024, Oprah Winfrey continued the saga of her on-again, off-again affair with dieting by producing a whole TV special on the subject.

By themselves, GLP-1 Agonists will not help you with your weight. If you want to lose weight, you must stick to a diet and exercise regimen, *combined* with one of these drugs.

Oh, Oh, Oh, Ozempic! is based on the pop song *Magic*, written in 1975 by David Paton and Billy Lyall of the group Pilot. Novo Nordisk, the manufacturer of *Ozempic,* started using it as a commercial jingle in 2018.

In 2025, one month's supply of Ozempic without insurance cost about $500.

How *manufactured* GLP-1 Receptor Agonist drugs work with the body's *natural* GLP-1s

An agonist is a manufactured substance that attaches to cell receptors and causes the same actions as a *naturally* occurring hormone—in this case GLP-1s.

In each of these **four GLP-1 events** below, *manufactured* Receptor Agonists, such as Ozempic, mimic and boost the actions of the *natural* GLP-1s.

Hundreds of GLP-1 drugs are in some stage of development. The first drug of this class was *Byetta,* developed in 2005. You had to inject it four times a day.

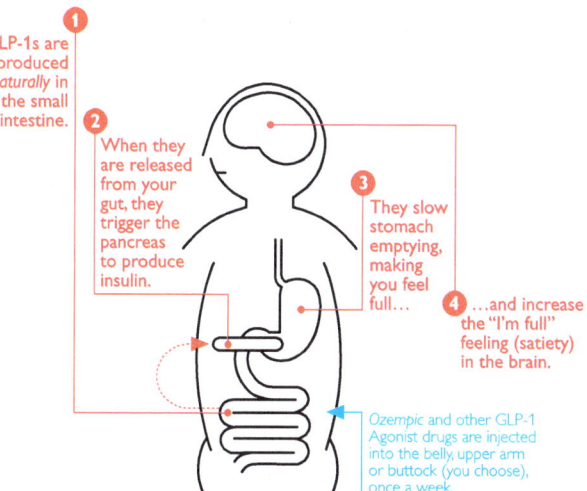

1 GLP-1s are produced *naturally* in the small intestine.

2 When they are released from your gut, they trigger the pancreas to produce insulin.

3 They slow stomach emptying, making you feel full...

4 ...and increase the "I'm full" feeling (satiety) in the brain.

Ozempic and other GLP-1 Agonist drugs are injected into the belly, upper arm or buttock (you choose), once a week.

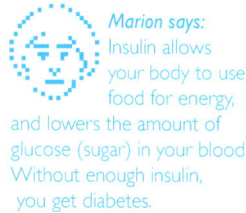

Marion says: Insulin allows your body to use food for energy, and lowers the amount of glucose (sugar) in your blood. Without enough insulin, you get diabetes.

There are many calculators online that do the math for you. (In the US, start with cdc.gov.) To calculate your BMI in pounds and inches, divide your weight by your height squared, then multiply by a conversion factor of 703. For example: weight 150lb, height 65in $[150 \div (65)^2] \times 703$ = 24.96 BMI

 Top heavy men

Top heavy men

William Howard Taft
6ft, 312lb
=42.3 BMI, extremely obese

Donald Trump
5ft 11in*, 240lb
= 33.47 BMI, obese

Theodore Roosevelt
5ft 10in, 210lb
=30.2 BMI, obese

* Not the height he'd like you to think, but carefully calculated from photo evidence.

How do you know if you are overweight?

In the 19th century, a Belgian astronomer and statistician, Adolphe Quetelet (←) founded the science of anthropometry, and invented the *Quetelet Index,* which today we call the Body Mass Index (BMI). Because Quetelet was measuring human norms and averages in an effort to establish and quantify the average human being, his work attracted the attention of the Eugenics movement, who regarded certain people—those outside the established norms—as undesirable.

But apart from that, there's a problem with the "averageness" of the BMI, and current disaffection with it is similar to negative opinions of the 10,000 steps per day idea (see page 66).

The BMI problem is this: because it's an estimate of fat in the body without making a difference between that and muscle, a person with minimal body fat and lots of muscle—a professional athlete, for instance, or just a really fit person—can have the same index number as an obese person with less muscle. And if you are very tall or very short, your BMI number will often be misleading.

The index originated in Europe, so your BMI number has traditionally been calculated in metric units. It's the result of dividing your weight, in kilograms, by the square of your height in meters. The resulting number will then fall into one of six groups that classify you as being somewhere between "underweight" and "extremely obese."

I have not peppered the chart (→) with actual BMI numbers because by themselves numbers don't mean as much to regular people as do the names of the groups. I mean, "overweight" is enough to make me think twice about that extra piece of chocolate, while "28" is not.

Also, Quetelet ranked the numbers for his "average" human adult according to his own observations, but we all know that while our height remains roughly the same, our weight varies from day to day, and that variation can nudge us from one group to another. According to this chart, on some days I have a "healthy weight," on other days I'm "overweight."

It seems to me that the BMI is "science" trying to impose a set of numbers on what is splendidly unique about humans: the mess of differences amongst us. Quetelet's average person reduces us all to one person. And that's a terrible thought. Vive la différence!

All that said, as long as you consider the limitations, BMI numbers *can* be useful as a generalized health guide, especially if you want to avoid the radiation involved with MRI or CT scans to get a detailed peek inside your body.

Try it for yourself here. (↓) No scary hospital visit necessary.

Another way to assess health risk is to measure our waists. 40in (102cm) for men, and 35in (90cm) for women indicates a higher than normal risk of heart disease, diabetes and liver problems—even if the BMI number is below the overweight range.

Source: Yale Metabolic Health and Weight Loss Program.

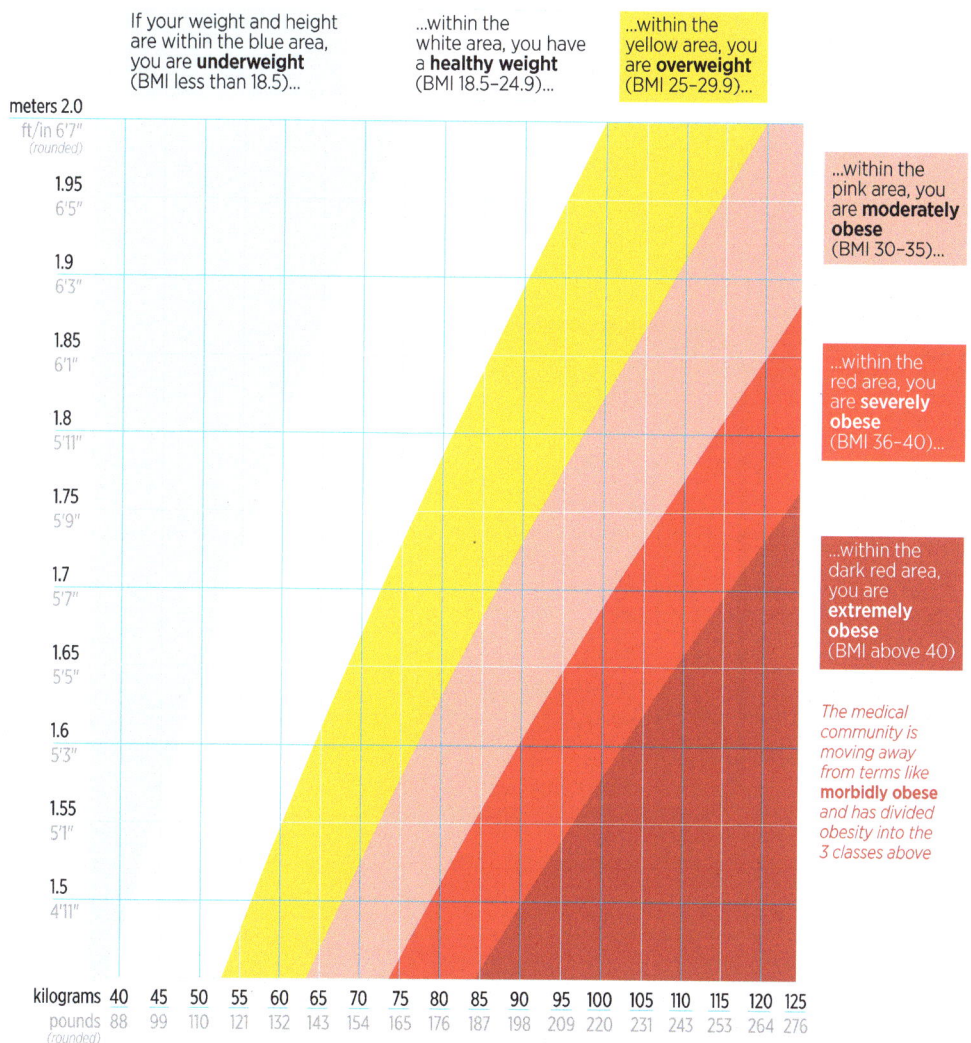

If your weight and height are within the blue area, you are **underweight** (BMI less than 18.5)...

...within the white area, you have a **healthy weight** (BMI 18.5-24.9)...

...within the yellow area, you are **overweight** (BMI 25-29.9)...

...within the pink area, you are **moderately obese** (BMI 30-35)...

...within the red area, you are **severely obese** (BMI 36-40)...

...within the dark red area, you are **extremely obese** (BMI above 40)

The medical community is moving away from terms like **morbidly obese** and has divided obesity into the 3 classes above

There'll be no fat-shaming here. I have too much of my own; in fact it's time for the unveiling of my pot belly—or more likely, my gin belly—the outline of which (↓) is faithfully traced off an embarrassing photo. My "official" BMI number puts me on the cusp of healthy and overweight, and I bet that belly is the culprit. I've had the ugly protrusion for a few years, and try to hide it with untucked shirts. When I gave up alcohol for 18 months, it went down, but not entirely. I do sit-ups in the gym, to little avail. Can I do anything about it in the gym? Apparently not— doctors say you can't crunch away a pot belly. I can only blame the amount of food I eat, the alcohol I drink—oh, that lovely sugar!—and sedentariness.

This diagrammatically arranged version of my insides shows the **two main kinds of fat** that can accumulate in the body:

 subcutaneous
(just under the skin)

 visceral
(inside the abdominal cavity).

 A comment from Dr. K
At med. school, we had anatomy books illustrated by F.H. Netter. The art was very realistic, but even so it wasn't nearly as bloody and messy as the real thing. A diagrammatic treatment is a better way to explain things, like this (→)..

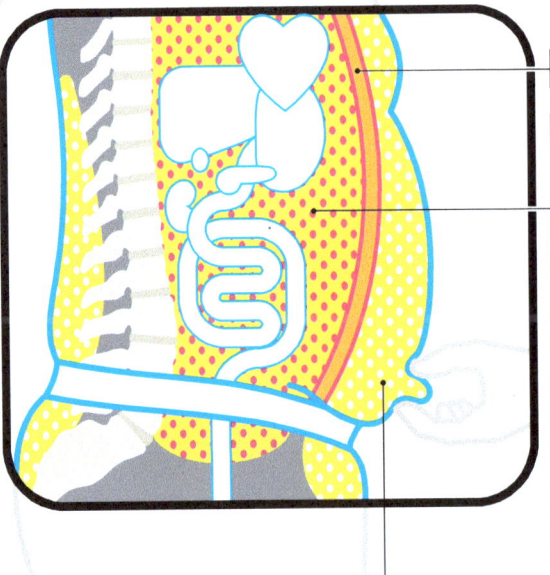

Abdominal muscle layer

Visceral fat
produces chemicals and hormones that are toxic, causing high blood pressure, diabetes, and heart disease. It is stored around *viscera*—heart, liver, gallbladder, pancreas, kidneys, intestines, and colon, and it occurs when you eat more calories than you burn.

Do you have it?
Your waist circumference is a good indicator—
Men: 37in (94cm)
Women: 31.5in (80cm)

Subcutaneous fat
is the squidgy stuff you can grab.

I asked my friend Richard Saul Wurman if he had anything to say about weight—his weight! He did.

You know who he is: creator of the TED, TEDMED and other conferences, and author/designer of 90+ books, including Information Anxiety, Mortality, *and the* Access *series of guidebooks.*

❝ My mother was chubby. My father was chubby. My brother was chubby. Well, I'm still alive. They're dead. I'll tell you two stories.

Story number one.

I was at dinner with my wife, Gloria, and Paul Prejza and his wife Deborah Sussman (famous for their 1984 design of the Los Angeles Olympics). Paul and I were jabbering away. Tubbiness, fatness, diet, came up in the conversation. Paul was overweight, but not as distended as I was. We said, let's see who could take off more weight. A competition thing was set up. We went to their office in Los Angeles and weighed each other. In two months, I'd go back to their office, and we would weigh ourselves again. Whoever took off the most weight could pick a restaurant and the loser would pay.

I wanted to win. I simply didn't eat. I basically subsisted on water.

I remember the morning of the appointed day. I drove to Santa Monica from Los Feliz and showed up at the scale where we would weigh each other. I remember for a while that morning I was in the bathroom spitting because I wanted to get any kind of liquid I could out of my body. I took off a significant amount of weight in those two months. Paul hardly lost anything because he hadn't taken the whole thing seriously. I won by 15lb.

We went out for an amazing dinner at Paul's and Deborah's expense at a wonderful restaurant in the Biltmore Hotel in LA.

Story number two.

There was an article on the front cover of *USA Today* about fatness, overeating, and losing weight. It had a little chart where you looked up your height, weight, whether male or female, and depending on where you were in the chart, it gave you a weight category—your BMI number. It said that I was "Morbidly Obese."

That really got to me. I thought I was a walking waddle of death. My doctor had never told me I was overweight. Of course, I knew I was overweight. Other people knew it. I saw it in their eyes. They mentioned it. I did the self-deprecation thing. I'm a short, fat, Jewish designer.

I had a company, The Understanding Business, shortened to TUB. It also stood for Archimedes' bathtub. When he got in and water went over the side, he said *Eureka*—I understood that! I'm a tub myself. I took that chart in *USA Today* to heart. I think if a doctor had said I was morbidly obese, or if I heard a whisper behind my back, it would have passed me by. But this newspaper story stuck. It was the moment I decided to eat less.

At that time, I weighed 276lb. Over the next nine or ten months, I weighed myself daily. I lost 100lb. Down to 176. No clothes fit me; my pants fell off. No diet, no exercise—just less food. I was noticeably a different person. People would say, oh my goodness, you've taken off a lot of weight. I would look them in the eyes, somberly. Pause. (Because silence is an extraordinary power when you're having a conversation.) Then I would say in a quiet voice, but not a whiny voice: *cancer.*

There was another silence. At this point I would walk away. Now, one shouldn't joke about cancer—one shouldn't do half the things I do. But I did that.

A last thought.

Today, I avoid putting food in front of me, and I realize that the first two bites of anything are the best, the last ten bites add nothing. For me, food is all about taste over quantity. ❞

4 Body, part 2. Fuel: what we put inside us

In 2010, during the Obama Administration, the White House arranged a meeting of nutritionists, food writers, designers, and advertising executives to discuss an update of the official US dietary guidelines, and to make recommendations for a new icon to replace the existing *MyPyramid* graphic. First Lady Michelle Obama was particularly interested—it was all part of her *"Let's Move!"* initiative, which addressed childhood obesity.

I was invited to the meeting because five years earlier, in response to the launch of *MyPyramid,* the newspaper *USA Today* had asked several graphic designers to consider the graphic (↓) and how it communicated recommendations for what to eat and how much. As designers, we weren't restricted to the pyramid shape, but were encouraged to make suggestions for graphic improvement, or do something completely different.

The 24 invitees included writers Michael Pollan (*Food Rules*), and Mark Bittman (*How to Cook Everything*); Jeff Goodby (his company created the "Got milk" ad campaign); Richard Saul Wurman (at that time he was running TEDMED, a medical offshoot of his TED conference); and my nutrition expert for this book, Marion Nestle.

MyPyramid appeared to be designed by committee: Let's have pictures! Let's have lots of color! Let's have an icon, and perspective! It did have a person climbing stairs—exercise added to diet, that was good—although the spiky climber would find very little to eat at the top of the pyramid. It did include the recommended proportion of each food group, but the triangular slices didn't show the data clearly enough.

MyPyramid was itself a new version of the original pyramid (↓) that had been in use since 1992.

My "redesigned" version is on the next page.

This (↑) was my answer to *USA Today*'s challenge. I tried to clarify the government's 2005 guidelines, showing the five food groups in the correct proportions needed for a healthy diet. Little tags confirmed the actual percentages of each group you should eat every day; on the web version, you would be able to click on them and get much more detail. When the graphic needed to be small, like a logo, I made a simplified version (←).

Before the 2010 White House meeting, we were sent relevant articles to read. As well as diet guidelines, it seemed clear from this material that some reference to exercise would be good in any suggestions about how *MyPyramid* might be updated, improved, or completely changed. (The brief was much the same as *USA Today*'s had been.)

I made a few quick sketches, based on my *USA Today* piece from five years earlier. When it came to my turn to present suggestions during the meeting, I explained that I was taking the exercise aspect of the assignment seriously, and literally: make the icon a 3-D object, not a graphic, by coloring a beach ball in the recommended proportions of the food groups. Kids could have fun and learn at the same time! Was it slightly tongue-in-cheek? It didn't matter, because no one seemed interested. The idea (↓) fell flat, and the meeting moved on to more serious ideas. I didn't say much more after that.

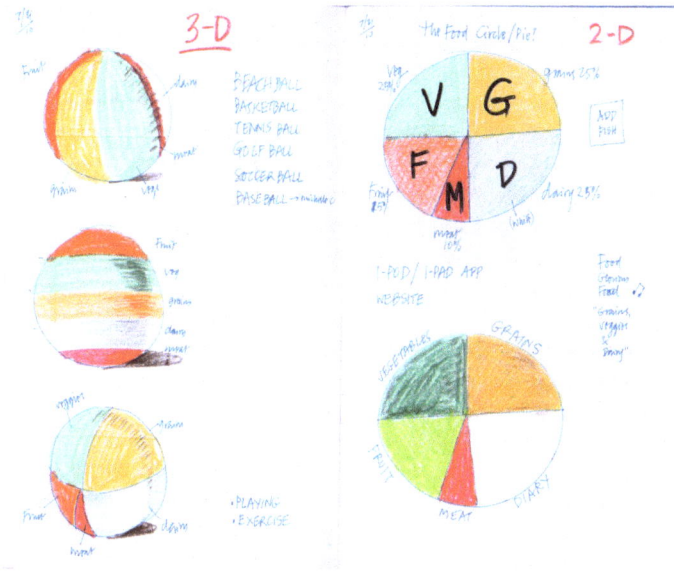

Almost a year passed. Then on June 2, 2011, the USDA unveiled the federal government's new food icon, *MyPlate* (↓). An excerpt from the press release:

United States Department of Agriculture.

"This is a quick, simple reminder for all of us to be more mindful of the foods that we're eating and as a mom, I can already tell how much this is going to help parents across the country," said First Lady Michelle Obama. *"When mom or dad comes home from a long day of work, we're already asked to be a chef, a referee, a cleaning crew. So it's tough to be a nutritionist, too. But we do have time to take a look at our kids' plates. As long as they're half full of fruits and vegetables, and paired with lean proteins, whole grains and low-fat dairy, we're golden. That's how easy it is."*

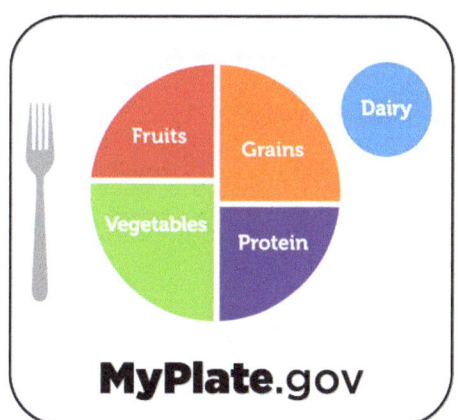

I was not involved in the design. But I was happy to see that the final icon was based on the newly recommended proportions of each food group. (And there was a nice little logo version, →.)

In her 2002 book, *Food Politics: How the Food Industry Influences Nutrition and Health*, my fellow White House invitee Marion Nestle had this advice: *Eat Less, Move More*. She stands by this today, but adds that if it was unpopular in 2002 because of the interests of Big Food, it's even more so now, but this time because of body politics—and the problem of obesity.

When we met to discuss her thoughts about nutrition for this book, I told her about a wonderful gift Erin and I were given for our wedding: a complete set of blue 1930s Depression glass— plates of all sizes, jugs, cups, and vases. We don't like huge helpings of food, but what we assumed were "dinner" plates in the set felt too small—instead, we use the oval serving platters as dinner plates. I suppose this means that we are part of the trend (at least in America) of wanting larger servings of food than people did in the 1930s.

Many US restaurants pile food on top of food— presumably thinking it represents value for money. But some are beginning to realize they can serve smaller portions, and that diners like it. (Not to mention it saves a whole lot of uneaten food that goes to waste.)

What's a serving size?

On nutrition labels, a "serving size" means how much of the product you must eat to properly get all the nutrients listed on the label—it's not the whole packet, box, or bottle. Here's what some serving sizes look like (actual size).

3 ounces of meat is about the size of a pack of cards

2 tablespoons of peanut butter: a ping pong ball

A "serving" of M&Ms: a shot-glass full (2 tablespoons)

1 ounce of cheese: 2 dice

What is ultra-processed food?

Serving sizes are just a part of the reason America's waists (and many of the world's) are expanding. Apart from people eating more in general, Big Food is working hard to make "food products" with ingredients that make them hard for us to resist, and also inexpensive—ultra-processed food. In 2019, Carlos Monteiro of the Department of Nutrition at the University of São Paulo and 11 colleagues published a paper that was designed to identify ultra-processed foods—defined within the NOVA classification system (→).

The paper says, "A practical way to identify an ultra-processed product is to check to see if its list of ingredients contains at least one characteristic of the NOVA ultra-processed food group, which is to say, either food substances never or rarely used in kitchens, or classes of additives designed to make the final product more palatable or more appealing."

NOVA has four categories: (a selection of foods on the lists →).
1. Unprocessed or minimally processed foods.
2. Processed culinary ingredients.
3. Processed foods made by combining foods from 1 and 2.
4. Ultra-processed foods made with industrial methods and ingredients not found in grocery stores.

According to Monteiro's paper, more than half of the calories consumed in high-income countries such as US, Canada, and the UK are ultra-processed foods, and a number of studies have been done to try to determine their harmful effects, resulting in observed links between ultra-processed foods and type 2 diabetes, obesity, and heart disease. This "food" is not real food. Read the labels and avoid as much of it if you can. (It's hard!)

Things to look for on nutrition labels and what they do
Sodium nitrates: stabilize, color, and flavor meat
Sulfites (sulfur dioxide, potassium bisulfite, sodium bisulfite, sodium sulfite): preservatives
Trans fats: improve shelf life of crackers and cookies
Monosodium glutamate (MSG): enhances flavor in Asian foods; soups
FD&C yellow #5 and #6: coloring agents in candy and cereal

Dr. Tera Fazzino from the University of Kansas uses the term *hyperpalatibility* to describe the phenomenon of not being able to resist eating more ultra-processed food than we need.

NOVA comes from the Portuguese *nova classificação* (new classification). The system was first proposed in 2009 by Monteiro and other researchers at the University of São Paulo.

Category **1** includes fresh or frozen fruits and vegetables, beans, meat, poultry, eggs, milk, plain yogurt, pasta, flour, coffee, tea, herbs, and spices.

Category **2** includes cooking oils, butter, sugar, honey, vinegar, salt.

Category **3** includes freshly baked bread, most cheeses, canned vegetables, beans, and fish.

Category **4** includes sodas and energy drinks, chips, candies, margarine, chicken nuggets, hot dogs, meat substitutes, and breakfast cereals.

A little bit about different dietary fats

Last year, a health scare eliminated my appetite. I barely took anything in for about ten days. If I ever needed an example, here it was: when you eat less, you lose weight. (And when you eat nothing, you lose a lot.) The body needs the right amount of

the three main macronutrient groups—carbohydrates, proteins, and fats—to give it energy (I lost that, too).

Conversely, if you eat *more* than you need (and don't exercise to work it off), naughty excess calories from fat sit like couch potatoes in your your body fat (adipose tissue). And not all dietary fats are good for your health.

Saturated fats include butter, cheese, whole milk, ice cream, fatty meats, coconut palm, and palm kernel oil. A diet high in saturated fat raises your LDL (bad) cholesterol, which clogs up your arteries and puts you at risk for heart-related and other health problems.

There are two kinds of **unsaturated fats**: *monounsaturated,* which include olive and canola oil, avocados, and certain nuts and seeds, and *polyunsaturated,* which include safflower, sunflower, corn and soy oil, walnuts, fish, and flaxseed. These fats can help lower your LDL cholesterol.

Apart from reading a product's nutrition label to see how much of these (→) fats it contains, beware of the **health halo** effect. It's a term that describes the perception that the food is healthy when its box or package claims it is "organic," "low calorie," "high in protein," or "vitamin fortified." There might be other ingredients that are less healthy—sugar, for instance, in a "protein" bar.

Hydrogenated fats, or **trans fats (trans fatty acids**) are unhealthy fats formed when vegetable oil goes through the hydrogenation process. They become solid at room temperature. These fats are often used to keep food fresh for a long time.

Despite the proliferation of diet fads, fundamental nutritional advice has not changed over the years. According to Marion Nestle: "In the 1950s, the first dietary recommendations for prevention of obesity, type 2 diabetes, heart disease and the like advised balancing calories and minimizing foods high in saturated fat, salt and sugar. The current US Dietary Guidelines urge the same."

Do diets work? Those who produce and market them say they do. But as many wellness writers (and economist Paul Krugman!) have said: *The best fitness and diet regimen is the one that you will actually follow.*

Sugar

The body needs sugar (a carbohydrate) for energy. Extra sugar is stored as fat (see over there ←), and too much of it leads to big health problems, obesity among them. I don't mean to preach, but there's too much sugar in our diets, even if we are not aware of it.

The average American consumes 19 teaspoons of sugar, every day

19 teaspoons

The American Heart Association recommends this:

6 teaspoons

actual size

60+ names for sugar appear on nutrition labels:

anhydrous dextrose, agave, agave nectar, beet sugar, brown sugar, cane juice solids, cane syrup, cane sugar, carob syrup, caster sugar, coconut sugar, confectioners' sugar, corn syrup, corn syrup solids, crystalline fructose, date sugar, demerara sugar, dextran, dextrose, dehydrated cane juice, evaporated cane juice, evaporated cane syrup, evaporated sugar cane, fructose, fructose crystals, fruit juice concentrate, glazing sugar, glucose, glucose syrup, golden syrup, granulated sugar, high-fructose corn syrup, honey, icing sugar, invert sugar, invert syrup, king's syrup, lactose, maple syrup, maple sugar, maltose, malt sugar, molasses, muscavado, nectar, pancake syrup, panocha, powdered sugar, raw sugar, refiners's syrup, sorghum, sorghum syrup, sucanat, sucrose, sugar, superfine sugar, table sugar, treacle, turbinado sugar, white sugar, yellow sugar

---

I wanted a more upbeat note to end this chapter on what we put inside our bodies, so…*behold beneficial broccoli!* Food and nutrition researchers have made extensive claims about the health benefits of this vegetable. Here's a selected list of why it's good for you:

- vitamins A, C, K, and B9 (folate)
- potassium
- phosphorus
- selenium
- antioxidants (support cells and tissues)
- bioactive compounds (reduce inflammation)

Research studies (some of them admittedly quite small) continue to examine broccoli's possible preventative superpowers. These include:

- protecting your skin from sun damage by UV radiation
- promoting healthy bones and joints (vitamin K and calcium)
- preventing osteoarthritis (sulforaphane)
- supporting a healthy immune system (vitamin C)
- promoting digestion (fiber and antioxidants)
- protecting against certain cancers, including breast, prostate, colorectal, bladder

Broccoli is a *cruciferous* vegetable, —a category of plants that comprises cabbage, Brussels sprouts, kale, and cauliflower. Have you ever looked closely at those cute eighth-inch (3mm) sprout-like buds?

You can eat broccoli raw or cooked, but don't overcook—it will lose valuable vitamin C.

FIVE 5

Move

Gently, at first.

If you have never exercised, or have lapsed and are currently out of shape, or if you are partially immobilized—perhaps after an injury—you can still get moving. Just go easy.

Sitting

Let's start with this: those of us who toil in front of a computer for hours should at least do this simple hand exercise (→).

This can help with carpal tunnel symptoms that are caused by repetitive motions. Make sure you are sitting upright with forearms and thighs parallel to the ground.

Then, try these, still sitting. (↓).

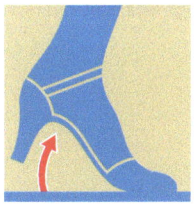
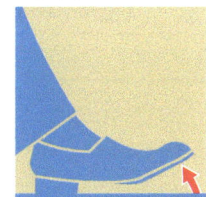
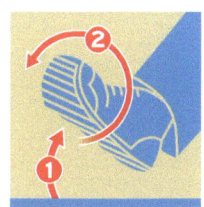

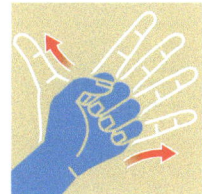
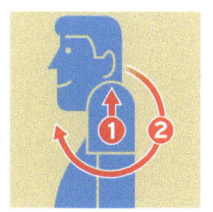

I drew these for an airline magazine—exercises to do on the plane, or waiting to board.

But do them anyway; a plane is not really necessary.

Sit-stand

Move the chair away from your computer, or sit on a dining chair. Put your right hand on your left shoulder, and the left hand on the right shoulder (←). Keep your heels close to the chair legs.

Set a timer for 30 seconds.

The Centers for Disease Control and Prevention (CDC), is part of the US government. It's a science-based, data-driven, service organization protecting the public's health.

Below, what the CDC thinks a healthy person should be able to do:

Men 65+ ... **12** times
under 65 ... **17** times

Women 65+ ... **11** times
under 60 ... **15** times

How many times can you stand up and sit down before the timer goes off?
Keep your hands on your shoulders all the time.

Standing
Now push the chair aside, and try a few upright exercises.

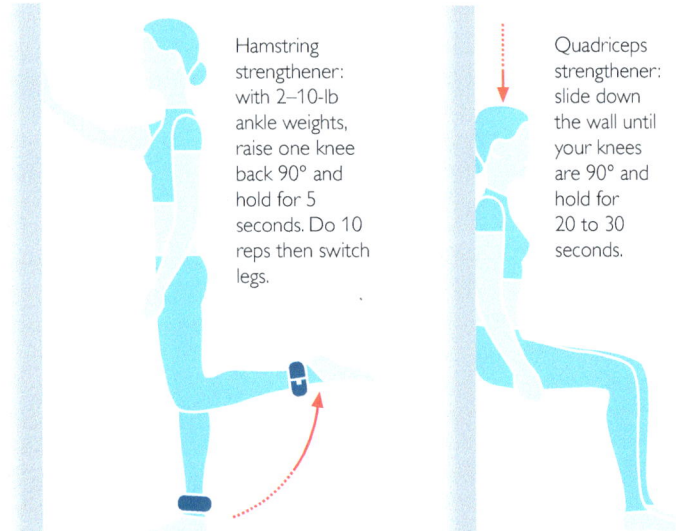

Hamstring strengthener: with 2–10-lb ankle weights, raise one knee back 90° and hold for 5 seconds. Do 10 reps then switch legs.

Quadriceps strengthener: slide down the wall until your knees are 90° and hold for 20 to 30 seconds.

These diagrams (→) and the ones on the next three pages were originally drawn for *Sports Illustrated for Women*. (Susan Casey, Art Director)

Quadriceps-gluteal strengthening lunge: step forward onto right leg, bringing weight forward as you bend it. Keep left heel off the floor. Hold for 20 to 30 seconds. Feel the stretch in the front of your left leg. Repeat with other leg.

Pull back and hold for 30 seconds.

Elastic straps come in a variety of strengths

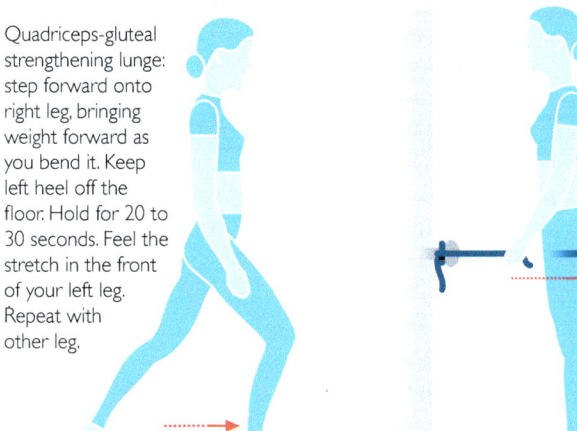

Run on the spot while swinging the ball (or a melon) from side to side.

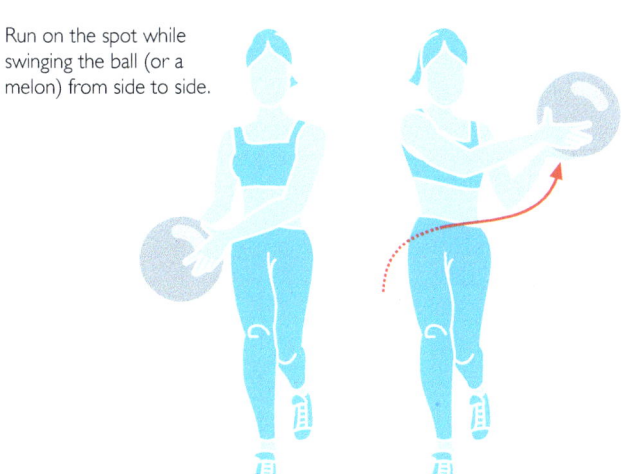

Raise right leg, bend back at the knee…

…and kick out. Repeat 3 times. Then do the same thing with the left leg.

Make sure there is no one next you (unless there is, and you are upset with them!)

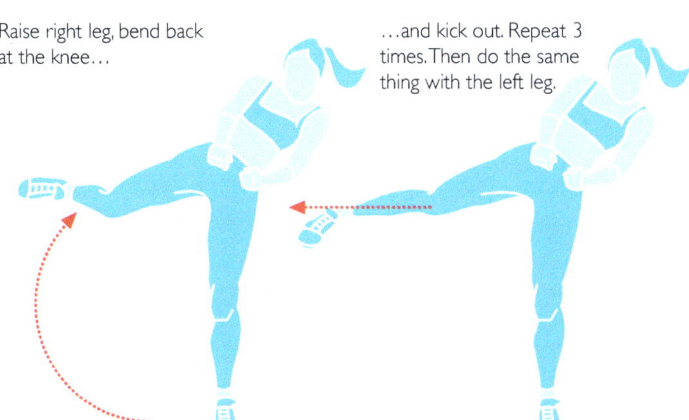

On the floor

Simple things you can do at home;
start with just a few reps.

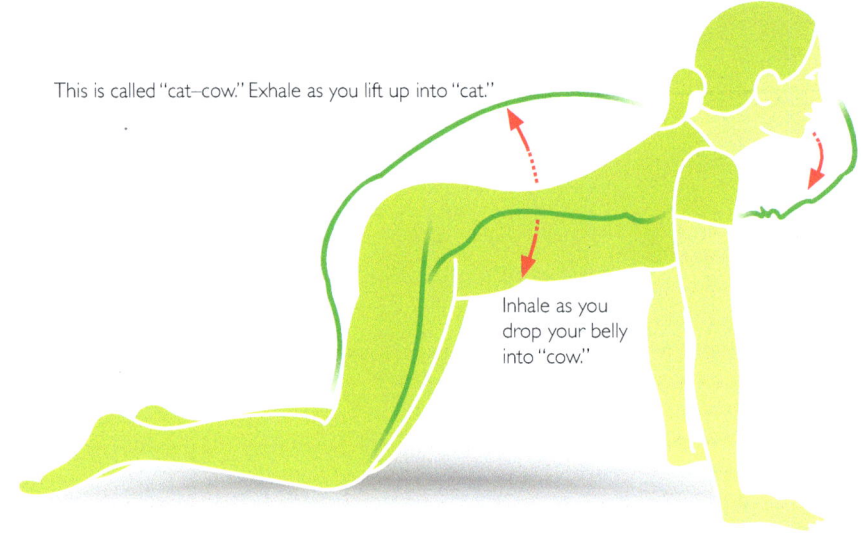

This is called "cat–cow." Exhale as you lift up into "cat."

Inhale as you drop your belly into "cow."

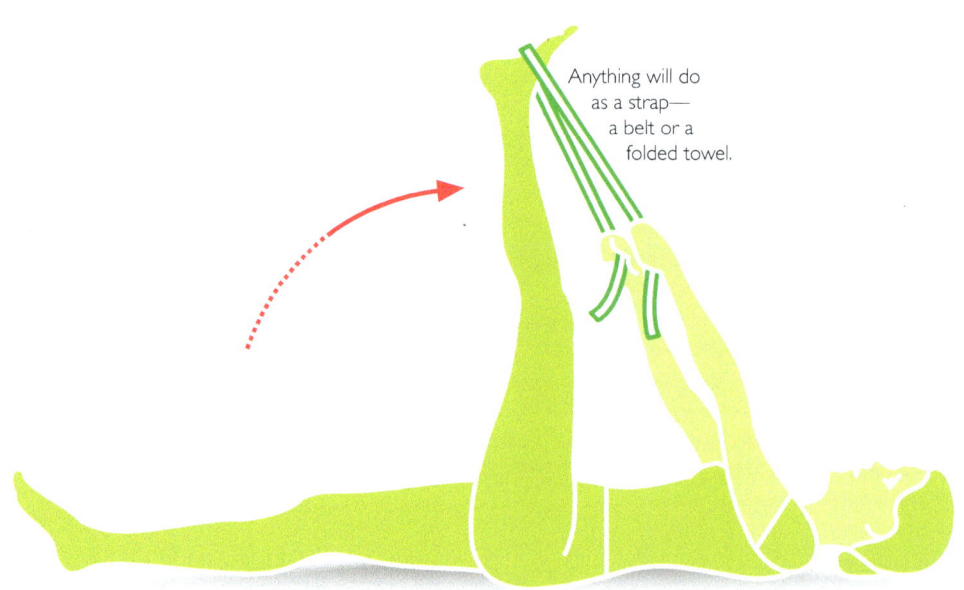

Anything will do as a strap— a belt or a folded towel.

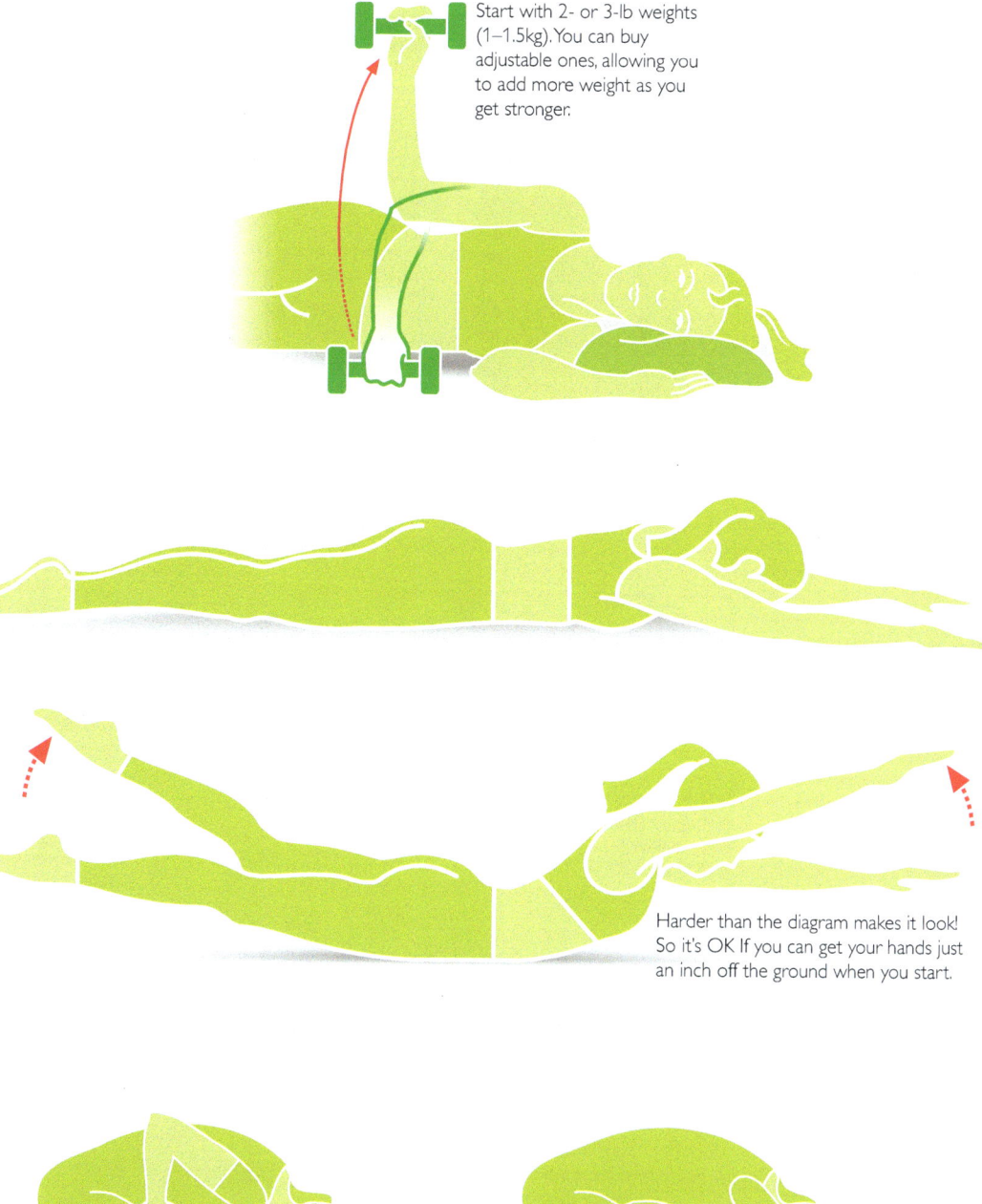

Start with 2- or 3-lb weights (1–1.5kg). You can buy adjustable ones, allowing you to add more weight as you get stronger.

Harder than the diagram makes it look! So it's OK If you can get your hands just an inch off the ground when you start.

This is relatively easy, but…

…this is more difficult. Try to make your head touch the floor.

This medieval thumbscrew was the kind of thing that you saw in the *Chamber of Horrors*.

OK, grammar people, when I was a youngster in London Madame Tussaud's had an apostrophe. Following a change of ownership in 2007, the apostrophe was dropped.

The basement *Chamber* itself was closed in 2016, but was recently reopened, with some of the more gory exhibits left out.

Into the gym

My first sight of the shiny, heavy, black, machines in the exercise rooms of my local YMCA (↓) reminded me of the torture devices encountered in the *Chamber of Horrors* below Madame Tussauds waxworks in London (←).

Many of the machines have helpful how-to graphics attached to them. But interestingly, the people depicted look about as realistic as Madame Tussauds wax models!

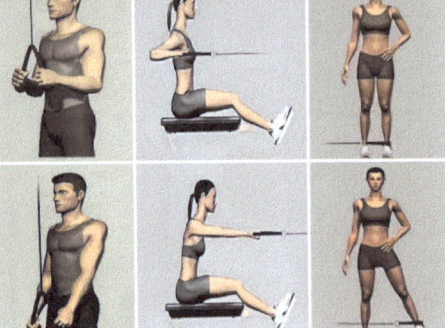

Q&A with my fitness expert, Gene DeNota

How long have you been a trainer?

I have been in the health and fitness industry since 1989. I have worn many hats since then, so I consider myself a fitness professional. My 9th grade science teacher owned the local health club—a tennis center, a pool, and a fitness area. So I got a job washing towels, racking weights and vacuuming the indoor tennis courts. I became a lifeguard, then moved into basic fitness instruction, and met a trainer who introduced me to a different gym, owned by a female bodybuilder—that's how my path into bodybuilding began. Eventually, I got into personal training. I turned 50 in January 2023, so I've been a fitness professional for quite some time!

What training methods have influenced you?

I always wanted to look like a Greek god, like Arnold! That's why I got into bodybuilding. I trained this way for many years—the single body part workout. I always wanted to be as strong as possible, so I incorporated powerlifting into my training. When I started personal training, I realized that not everyone wanted to be a bodybuilder. So I had to learn new methods, like split body workouts. HIIT (high intensity interval training) is a method that I use, especially when teaching group classes.

My current workout routine varies from week to week, and season to season. I have a love/hate relationship with golf. So when the weather is nice, you can find me on the golf course. I try to lift weights 3-4 times a week, and I incorporate cardio and conditioning 2-3 times a week.

Why do people come to you?

Most of the clients I train are for general fitness, but all have a specific underlying goal, and some have weight loss goals. I have trained clients for specific sports or events. I helped a client prepare for a marathon; others who were preparing for police, fire, and FBI fitness tests. I train a 60-year-old man who can run circles around some of my younger male clients. Currently I have clients who play tennis and golf. We work on movements specifically geared to their sport. I've also trained people specifically for bodybuilding and physique competitions. Those are the most challenging, and the most rewarding.

What are the biggest mistakes people make in the gym?

I find that the biggest mistakes people make are: one, not asking for help; two, thinking they know more than they actually do, perhaps because they were once a college athlete; three, believing that social media influencers and YouTube fitness videos are the answer!

Tell me about machines vs. free weights.

They both serve a purpose and should be incorporated into all workouts. Machines isolate some muscles a little better and can be safer for beginners. Free weight exercises can force more muscles to engage in a exercise.

How often should we exercise? Can we overdo it?

As a minimum, I recommend exercising 30 minutes, three times a week. With a healthy diet, this will keep you right where you are, not much gained, and not much lost (but if that's all you can do, it's a lot better than nothing). If you really want to make a change in your health and fitness, then I recommend 45-60 minutes a day, five days a week. Within that, at least three days of strength training is important. Cardiovascular training should be broken up into low intensity and high intensity—both have a very different benefit.
All this said, if your workouts are not properly formatted, you can overdo it. Yes, there is such a thing as overtraining.

TGU x 3
- - - - - - -
10 x DL
5/5 x C/S/P
10 x GUSU
5/5 x SNATCH/REV LUNGE
20 x Swings/FIG 8
- - - - - - -
TGU x 3

Trainers write their exercise routines on the gym walls. They each have a personal vocabulary!

Rotate after 20

I like this one, involving two people throwing a weighted ball to each other, while a third person does burpees between them.

*I won't say
a word.*

Heavy metal

Why are they called "dumbbells"? (←)

In the centuries before gym equipment was developed, would-be fitness freaks had to improvise. Joseph Addison (1672–1719) concocted a rope and weight pulley. It was like pulling the rope in a church to make the bell chime. But since there was no bell, just a heavy weight, it was a dumb bell. Addison said: *"I exercise myself for an hour every morning upon a dumb bell, in profound silence."*

English poet and politician. (An unlikely combo today.)

 With his friend Richard Steele, Addison founded *The Spectator* magazine, which was about politics, not watching sports.

And why "kettlebells"? (←)

First used in the Soviet Union, they have a less obvious etymology—or perhaps not: the origin of the name may simply be that they look like kettles without a spout.

William of Ockham (Occam) would go with this answer.

What are "Burpees"? (↓)

The exercise is named after US physiologist Royal Huddleston Burpee, Sr., who invented it in 1939. It became popular when the US Army made it one of the ways to measure the fitness of WWII recruits. These are the basic steps:

There are many variations. For instance, in the third position above—plank—you might lower your chest to the floor, then return to the squat position. The fifth position could be a vertical jump with arms raised, before starting the whole routine again. If you played football (in the US), you know this as an "up-down."

World Burpee records

One minute: 38 chest-to-ground Burpees by Philippe Jouan, on April 29, 2023, in Quebec.

One hour: 951 chest-to-ground Burpees by Cassiano Laureano, on June 25, 2021, in Singapore.

And why are they called "medicine" balls? (→)

"Medicine" describes anything that heals the body after an accident. Weighted balls were first used by Persian wrestlers to make them stronger, and the Father of Medicine, Hippocrates, filled leather balls with sand to help build strength. In 1931, White House physician Admiral Joel T. Boone invented *Hoover-Ball*, to keep President Hoover fit. The game was played by teams of two or four, with a 6lb ball over an 8-foot high net.

In 1824, James Hardie wrote *The History of the Tread-Mill*. It's about the use of the machine as hard labor—an alternative, in the US, to the death sentence for crimes such as piracy, treason and mail robbery. The most common use of the treadmill was to grind corn, so prisoners were being productive while being punished. These old treadmills were not flat like home machines, they were more like the stairmaster machines you see in gyms, making the prisoners' punishment more punishing.

I've used *Rover* as a generic dog name; it could have been *Fido* or *Spot*. Here are the equivalent stereotypical doggie monikers from other countries:
Bluey—Australia
Bobi—Portugal
Bran—Ireland
Burek—Poland
Foofoo—Thailand
Jim—New Zealand
Luna—Spain
Maks—Croatia
Morzi—Hungary
Musti—Finland
Pochi—Japan
Quiaokeli—China
Raoul—France
Simba—Kenya

Mitchell Rudy set a Guinness World Record when he walked 38 dogs at one time, in South Korea. The dogs came from *Korean K9 Rescue*, a non-profit that finds homes for abused and stray dogs. After the kilometer (half a mile) walk he said, "my arms felt like they were on fire."

Beyond the gym: Walking

Walking has been shown to be great low-impact exercise. When the weather's good, you can go for a walk outdoors and enjoy the sun, but if you simply cannot tear yourself away from the drawing board (or if it's snowing and no sun), you can walk *and* work, using an under-desk treadmill. Some manufacturers call their machines walking pads, which sounds more friendly, especially when you know a bit about what was called the *Tread-Mill* (←) in the 19th century. As with any 21st-century fitness equipment, there's a big range of prices, starting around $150. You can find nicely portable lightweight models, but they all assume that you'll be upright at your desk, not sitting, so you'll need an adjustable-height desk (→).

Now let's say you're ready to go for a walk outside, and Rover is wagging his tail in anticipation of coming, too. Then it snows! No problem: while you step back onto your new under-desk walking pad, Rover gets onto his own doggie-mill. (→) (It will probably cost about twice as much as your machine, but it keeps him fit, right?)

If you want to give Rover a real workout, you could get a hamster-wheel dog treadmill. Yes, it's a thing (←). Just don't tell him about its 19th century antecedent.

Much has been written about the emotional value and life-lengthening effect that dogs have on their owners. (There's also a comparable amount of studies debunking the theories.)

But if walking the dog gets you moving, do it! You might even take other peoples' pets out with you, and be on your way to a whole new profession!

No dog to nudge you on? Try these:
walking with weights…

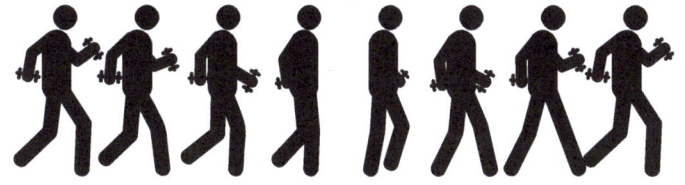

You could also put on a backpack with some books in it—but don't carry too much (see next page).

…faster…

And perhaps extend your range—go a little farther, as well as faster.

…in a group…   …backward? (You'll get funny looks.)

…uphill

…even be *silly*, like John Cleese in *Monty Python's Flying Circus*.

Next, much longer walks.

Hiking: lighten up!

Yes, you need a backpack, maps and
a compass, a first aid kit, food and water.
But if you carry less you'll keep
going much longer.

See
what
happens
when you
you take
a load
off your
back.

**2.5kg
(5lb)**

**4.5kg
(10lb)**

**11.5kg
(25lb)**

Uneven ground plays havoc with
your legs, adding pressure on your
knees. When you lighten your load
your knees will thank you.

What stuff weighs

- Depending on its capacity, the backpack itself should be light. There are packs with enough room for a three-day hike starting around 0.5kg (15oz).

- sleeping bag 0.5kg (16oz) ● sleeping pad 0.25kg (9oz) ● tent 1.5kg (3.3lbs).

- rain gear 0.3kg (10oz) ● stove 0.06kg (2oz) ● fuel 0.2kg (7oz)

- Take food out of the packaging it comes in, and put it into plastic bags.

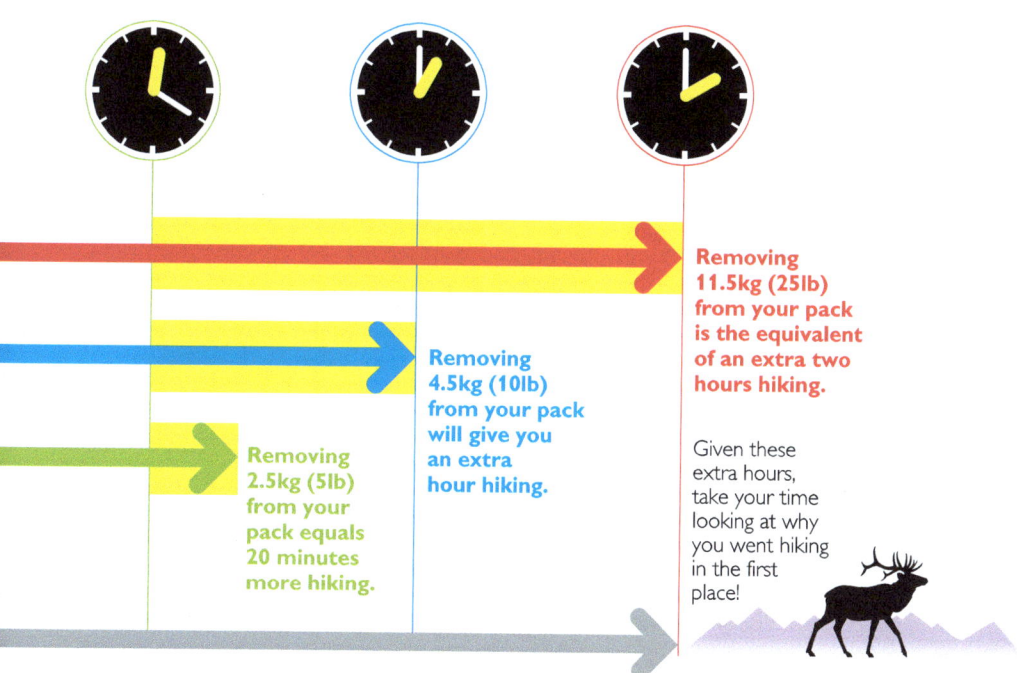

Removing 2.5kg (5lb) from your pack equals 20 minutes more hiking.

Removing 4.5kg (10lb) from your pack will give you an extra hour hiking.

Removing 11.5kg (25lb) from your pack is the equivalent of an extra two hours hiking.

Given these extra hours, take your time looking at why you went hiking in the first place!

Next, what's all the fuss about taking 10,000 steps every day? (→).

Why take 10,000 steps?

Dr. I-Min Lee, an epidemiologist at Harvard Medical School, traced the origin of 10,000 steps to 1965 when a Japanese company, *Yamasa Clock,* created a pedometer called *Manpo-kei* ("10,000 steps meter") because the Japanese character for 10,000 looks a bit like a person walking (↓). Basically, it was a marketing gimmick.

In 2019, Dr. Lee published a study about the physical activity and health of 16,741 women aged 62 to 101. Many subsequent articles about the subject refer to this study, but often don't mention that the participants were all women, while nevertheless using the study's findings to bolster arguments about the benefits or otherwise of taking 10,000 steps— regardless of gender or age.

The original 1965 device that recorded users' steps was worn on the waist, not on the wrist (as is the case with *Fitbits* and the like), or in a pocket (as with a smartphone). This made the *Manpo-kei* pedometer an accurate step counter. An algorithm in today's fitness devices translates arm swings into steps taken (with information from three accelerometers), and that's why you are directed to input your height, weight, and age before you start using the new fitness gismos.

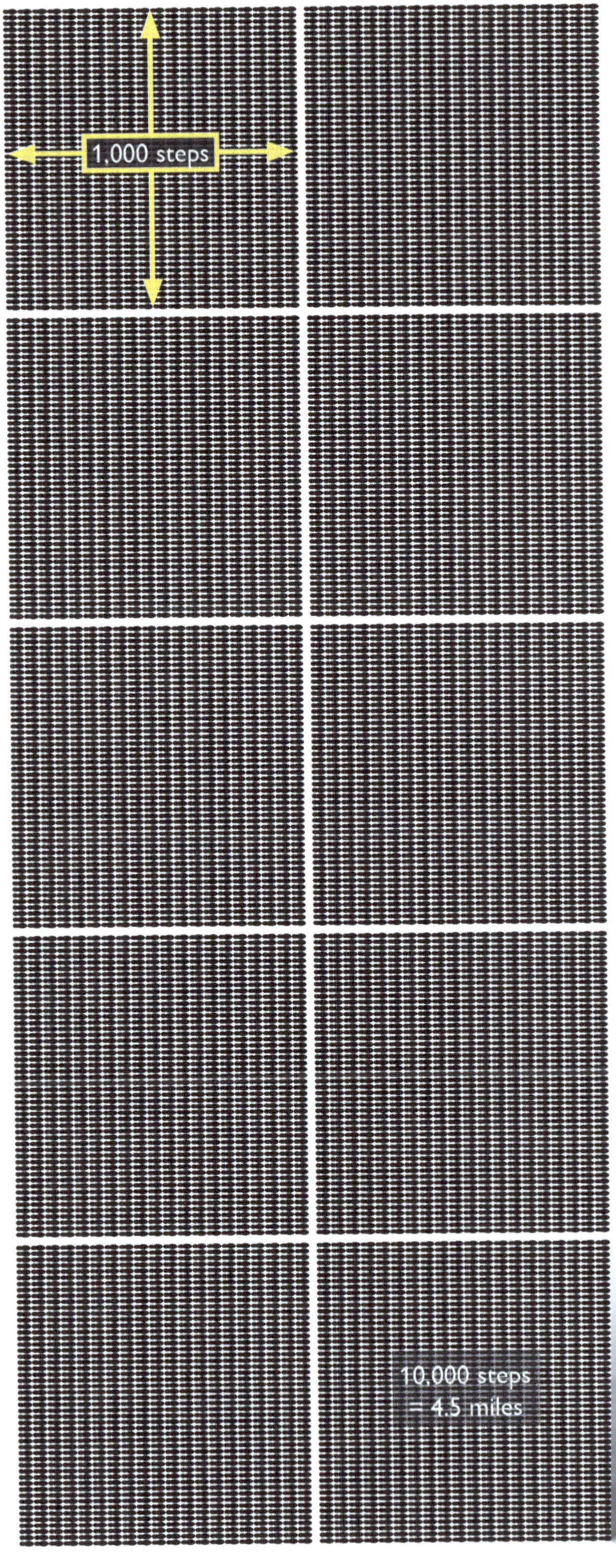

1,000 steps

10,000 steps = 4.5 miles

Are there any health benefits in taking 10,000 steps a day?

There are none according to Dr. Lee's study. Participants wore a pedometer on their hips for seven days (while they were awake) between 2011 and 2015, with a follow-up four years later, at which time the data was analyzed and published. The study showed that as few as 4,400 steps were "significantly related to lower mortality rates," and that taking more than 7,500 steps had no extra beneficial effect.

Dr. Lee reminded us that her study was limited to women aged 62 and older, and that she was interested in mortality rather than anything to do with quality of life or general physical and mental fitness. Of course, *any* physical activity is good for you, but beware of fitness theories; they often contain a great deal of *galimatias*, and plenty of *vlother*. (I don't know enough to question the validity of Dr. Lee's study, so I hope you won't accuse me of *sciolism*.)

Well, I'll leave it to you to decide whether you want to embrace the *Manpo-kei* idea. Just please remember that a total of 4,400 daily steps (↓), as recorded by your accelerometer, has been shown to be enough to help you keep fit, and you don't need to take 10,000 steps a day. Which is a relief, because in the interest of good

Complete list of the study's authors: I-Min Lee, MBBS, ScD; Eric J. Shiroma, ScD; Masamitsu Kamada, PhD; David R. Bassett, PhD; Charles E. Matthews, PhD; Julie E. Buring, ScD.

 Word nerd alert! Wonderful examples of old words to describe nonsense:
Galimatias (intellectual poppycock)
Vlother (balderdash)
Sciolism (the pretense of having a deeper understanding of a topic about which one has only a shallow understanding)

All from *Grandiloquent Words* by Jason Travis Ott.

 Charles Dickens—who may well have used those wonderful words above—walked 12 miles every day, and sometimes 20, through the poorer parts of London. On his longer trips, Ye Olde Fitbit would be announcing more than 50,000 steps. David Sedaris (see next page) would be proud.

research, I thought I should try the 10,000-step program, and bought a wrist pedometer—after all, here I am writing about them. I charted 31 days of my steps (→). After filling out my height and weight in the accompanying (and necessary) smartphone app, the device immediately suggested that, given the details I had entered, I actually needed to take *11,000* steps every day. I only exceeded that number once—when my wife and I shoveled snow for four hours.

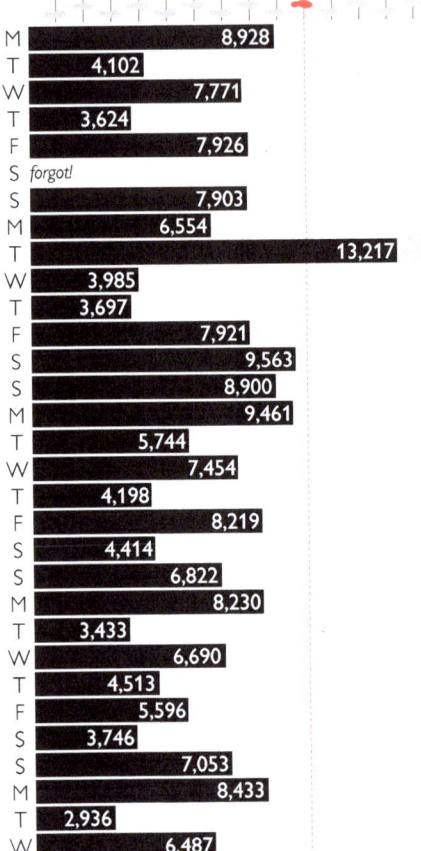

		10k
M	8,928	
T	4,102	
W	7,771	
T	3,624	
F	7,926	
S	*forgot!*	
S	7,903	
M	6,554	
T		13,217
W	3,985	
T	3,697	
F	7,921	
S	9,563	
S	8,900	
M	9,461	
T	5,744	
W	7,454	
T	4,198	
F	8,219	
S	4,414	
S	6,822	
M	8,230	
T	3,433	
W	6,690	
T	4,513	
F	5,596	
S	3,746	
S	7,053	
M	8,433	
T	2,936	
W	6,487	

Marion says: When I look at this chart, I can see you own a car! I divide my time between Ithaca, NY, and New York City. No one has a car in the city. When I'm there, there's hardly ever a day when I am *not* walking 10,000 steps. My partner is 92, and he does between 4,000 and 6,000 steps a day.

As you can see, a more usual total for my day was between roughly 3,500 and 8,000 steps, the higher numbers reflecting days I went to the gym, which typically consisted of treadmill walking for 15 minutes, rowing machine for five minutes, resistance training and stretching for 40 minutes. On other days, I sat at a computer writing this; walked over to the fridge a few times; and went on an occasional shopping errand. The average American takes between 5,000 and 7,000 steps per day (burning off one calorie for each 20 steps), so I suppose I am finally an average American!

The device I used had cute animated graphics (←), but the idea of being attached to another digital thing is the opposite of my idea of happily staying fit. It's not fun to be stalked all day, only to fall short of the attentive algorithm's expectation when checking the number of steps for the day before turning out the light at night. So I let my waking hours be monitored for a month, and then stopped and went back to living an untracked life again. I have my own biased opinion about counting steps, but, whatever gets you going is good, and we *do* love our gadgets—I see lots of devices at the gym, with their owners insistently poking at them.

I watched the 2024 solar eclipse. It was 90% obscured where we live in the Northeast US, and apart from being amazed at how light it remained when 90% of the sun was hiding behind the moon, I day-dreamed about how many steps it would take to walk to the moon—and when I'd get there—using my *Fitbit,* of course.

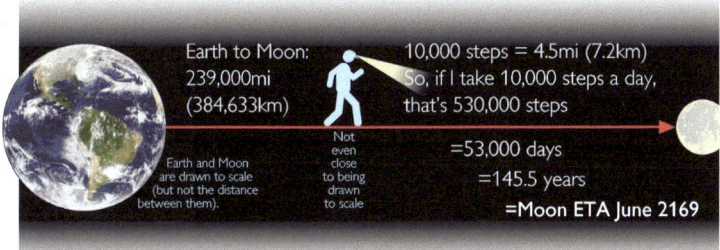

Earth to Moon: 239,000mi (384,633km)

Earth and Moon are drawn to scale (but not the distance between them).

Not even close to being drawn to scale

10,000 steps = 4.5mi (7.2km) So, if I take 10,000 steps a day, that's 530,000 steps

=53,000 days
=145.5 years
=Moon ETA June 2169

I foresee a couple of logistical questions about this endeavor.

Famous Fitbit fan

David Sedaris (→), the renowned and very funny writer has detailed his use of the *Fitbit* tracker: *"I'm completely obsessed. It's like a sickness; I've been Fitbit-ten...".* He gradually worked up from 10,000 daily steps to many more, musing on days that he averaged only 30,000: *"Honestly, how lazy can you get?...now I'm up to 60,000 which is twenty-five and a half miles...walking that distance takes close to nine hours."* Readers, be warned—if you read books while you are on a stationary bicycle at the gym (or at home), please DON'T read *his* books. You'll fall off the machine laughing, probably injuring yourself. And fellow fitness fanatics (or your cat) will think you've gone mad.

Sedaris wrote about his love affair with the *Fitbit* in *Stepping Out,* one of the essays in his 2018 book, *Calypso (originally published in The New Yorker).*

Something else: since it seems that the whole world is hopelessly addicted to electronic gadgets, why not consider the **walking phone call**? Instead of sitting at your desk, turn long phone meetings into mini exercise routines. Get fit while listening to the latest boring, but mandated, corporate update. (Of course you can blame the phone when it cuts you off...sort of accidently on purpose.)

Next, runnnnnnnnnnnnning.

Running

Stories about famous runners often start with the legend of Pheidippides, who was said to have run from Marathon to Athens in 490 BC, carrying a message that the Greeks had won a great victory over the Persians. Legend has it that as he arrived in Athens, he screamed *nike! nike!* (the Greek word for *victory*), and dropped dead on the spot. It may not be true (←).

My list of running heroes includes Jesse Owens, who won four gold medals at the Berlin games in 1936; Roger Bannister, who was the first person to run a mile in under four minutes (1954);

Who invented the marathon? It's not as ancient as you think, by Erin Blakemore: While there were foot races at the ancient Olympics, they weren't marathons. What's more, at the 1896 games, held in Athens—the first modern Olympiad—the run was 24.85 miles, which was the distance from Marathon to Pnyx (near Athens). Then in 1908, at the London Olympics, the race was extended to 26.2 miles, and it's been that way ever since.

Running appears to be a gift to idiom lovers: *in the short run; in the long run; run rings around; run amok; run for one's money; runs in the family; run its course; run it up the flagpole; run like clockwork; running on empty; run of the mill; run out of steam; running battle; run the gauntlet; run that by me again.*

This is the classic heel-toe running style. But there's nothing wrong with leading with your toes rather than your heels, if that's what feels natural.

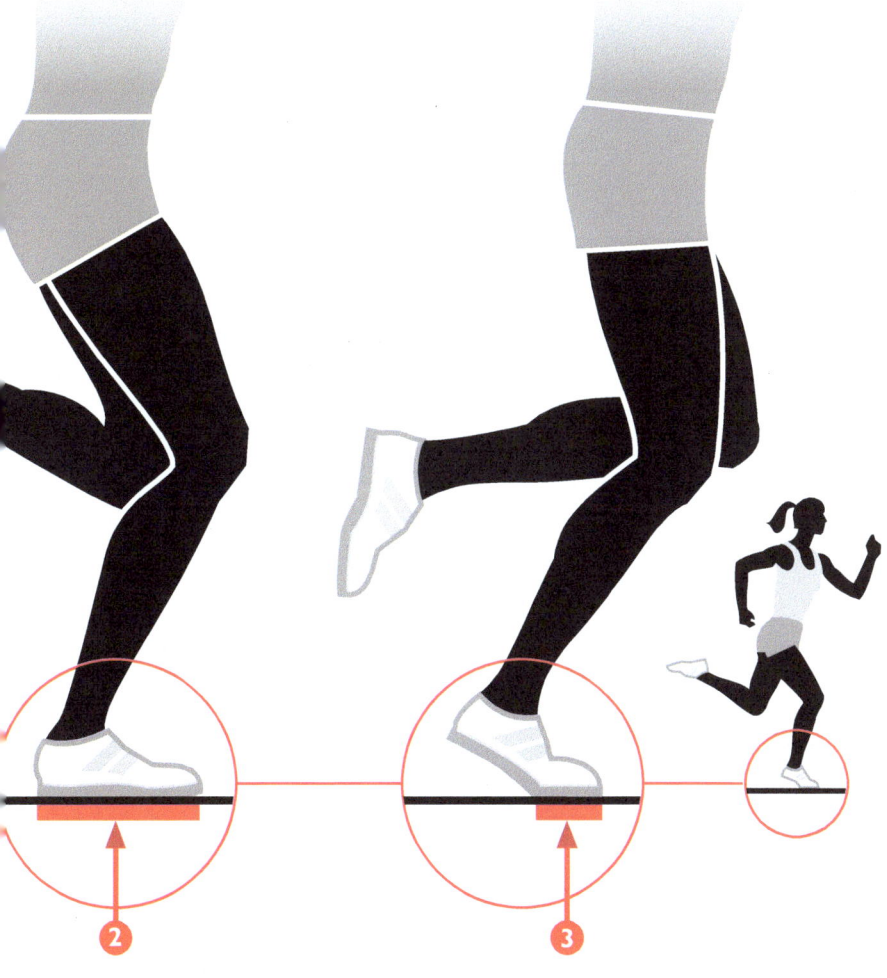

and Usain Bolt, who, in 2009 ran 100 meters in 9.58 seconds—a speed of 23.35 mph (37.58kph)—making him at that time the fastest man on Earth. I think about that when I struggle to reach 18 mph (29kph) on my power-assist bike.

As with many exercises, people differ about the "best" way to run, whether you are casually doing it, or more seriously training for a 5K race, or even a marathon.

There does seem to be agreement about the so-called fast-slow approach. In Sweden, the term is *Fartlek* ("speed play"), where a

Fartlek was developed in the 1930s by Gösta Holmér.

runner alternates spurts of sprinting with much slower periods of running. Running as fast as you can is excellent aerobic *and* anaerobic exercise, because it uses oxygen to meet the energy demands of exercise (aerobic), while also building muscle strength by breaking down glucose in the body, *without* using oxygen (anaerobic).

Long-distance running

Let's do the Marathon! might sound good as a drunken bet or a dare, but it's not a good idea to attempt a 26+ mile race without quite a bit of training! A major consideration: running shoes.

A new genre of shoes—unsurprisingly called *Supershoes*—is designed to help you endure the rigor of marathons and half-marathons. They include a stiff midsole made of carbon fiber (dotted line above) which stores energy from the shoe's flex when you first hit the ground, and it transforms that flexion into a springy boost as you lift back off.

Here's a fast shoe! The L.L. Bean *Bootmobile* (↓) can reach 65mph.

Nike's *Alphafly* (↑), drawn actual size (US 9), is considered one of the best new shoes. In this drawing, what looks like a cutaway is

actually visible on the shoe itself, showing a key part of its structure, and why *Supershoes* have become popular. Nike calls it an *"Air Zoom"* unit. There are two at the front of each shoe, cushioning impact with the road and returning energy back to the runner, (adding to the extra energy from the carbon fiber midsole).

The Kenyan runner Kelvin Kiptum was wearing *Alphaflys* when he set the Marathon World Record (2:00:35) in October, 2023, in Chicago. It was assumed that Kiptum would be the first person to run a Marathon in under two hours, but he died at age 24 in a car accident in Kenya, in 2024.

The Marathon problem We store between 1,800 and 2,000 calories-worth of glycogen in our muscles and liver. On average, a runner will use up 100 calories per mile, so it's easy to understand why the sensation of "hitting the wall" (↓) often happens at the 18- or 20-mile (30k) mark in a marathon. When it happens, you have to slow down. Your muscles are now burning more fat than glycogen. Those muscles *will* work, just slower—despite "go-faster" messages your brain keeps sending down to your legs.

Did Pheidippides hit the wall, during his run from Marathon to Athens in 490 BC?
We don't know.

HITTING THE WALL In any activity using muscles, it's your brain that's doing the thinking, but it may not seem that way when your legs stop working.

1 Your brain sends electrical impulses to the muscles, signaling them when to spring into action.

2 To be able to work, muscle cells need energy, which is stored as glycogen (a carbohydrate).

3 Glycogen fuels the conversion of ADP (Adenosine Diphosphate) to ATP (Adenosine Triphosphate) which provides energy to mitochondria, tiny organisms inside muscle cells.

4 Your available supply of ATP is used up in one second—one stride— so to continue running, your body must keep renewing the supply.

5 When the supply of ATP is low, muscles don't get enough to cover energy needs, and they don't work as fast as you want them to.

You've hit the wall.

Long-distance cycling

The Paris-Brest-Paris (PBP) race is the oldest cycling event in the world. It started in 1891 with professional riders—riding bikes with wooden wheels, on dirt roads—and was held every five years until 1951, when it ceased to be an competitive race. It is still held as a non-professional event, every four years, with a goal of completing the 1,200km (750 miles) course (→) in 90 hours. There are rigorous pre-event qualifying rides (200, 300, 400, and 600km) for anyone wanting to take part. These are run by cycling clubs around the world. You can't compete if you don't have proof.

The next PBP is in 2027.

My friend Peter Dobyns did the ride in 2007, with his friends Hauke Kite-Powell, and Garth Hoffman, and with 5,000 other riders. (In recent years, the number of riders has grown to a maximum of 8,000.) To cope with the numbers, riders start off in waves; Pete, Hauke, and Garth had to wait until 11pm. They left Paris in a drenching rain that lasted for almost the entire three and a half days that they were on the road. Pete's main food was five dried apricots munched at regular intervals. (That's 110 calories—easy to digest, without leaving too much in the stomach—while supplying needed energy to his legs.) He told me it was such an intense event, that his thought process was compromised. He felt his brain shutting down.

One of Peter's fellow participants was an old gentleman wearing a top hat, riding an anciet bike with a gas lantern and just two gears.

Here's Pete's sister Shelley who, with their father Frank, accompanied Pete and his fellow riders in a support vehicle—a nine-seater van they slept in for three nights:

"Support vehicles were not allowed on the same roads as the cyclists; Frank was the navigator, and I did the driving. We fought a lot! We had a few hours to kill while "the boys" reached each control point, so we looked for hot food they'd like. At one control point near Paris on the return from Brest, Peter couldn't take any food, was shivering from the cold and almost incessant rain, and looked so gray that I thought he was going to die."

I asked Hauke to give me his thoughts on the ride:

"I had ridden the PBP three times before this one, and now at age 62, I haven't ruled out doing it again. Training for it is lengthy and difficult, and although my knees still are good to go, the hardness of that little seat is tough on your bottom! In Europe, long-distance riding is quite common among 50-, 60-, and 70-year-olds who have aged out of competitive cycling, and many people on this ride were of those ages."

"We rode at 14-15mph (22-24kph) and got back to Paris in just over 86 hours, but some hardcore riders—who completed the course in about 40 hours—would be cycling at 20mph (32kph). They would eat while they rode, and stop only for bathroom breaks. I saw a couple of them going the opposite way to us—back to Paris. We were in it for fun (and proud to be able to finish).

Almost all of the route is on country roads that are used by farmers and their cattle. The combination of cowshit and heavy rain meant that the bikes and our bodies and goggles were spattered all over with muck. But even through the night, villagers would come out and cheer us on.

Shelley and Frank were a phenomenal support group, meeting us at each control stop, which were spaced about 50km apart along the route. We had to have our cards stamped at each one. Then we'd typically have something to eat, and afterwards sleep for about four hours in the van, before starting off again. We got medallions at the finish. (That reminds me, I must find mine!)"

Mountain biking is very different from long-distance. (You don't go nearly as far!) And you are on a more rugged machine in a more upright position. Here are a few things to watch out for on your mountain bike.

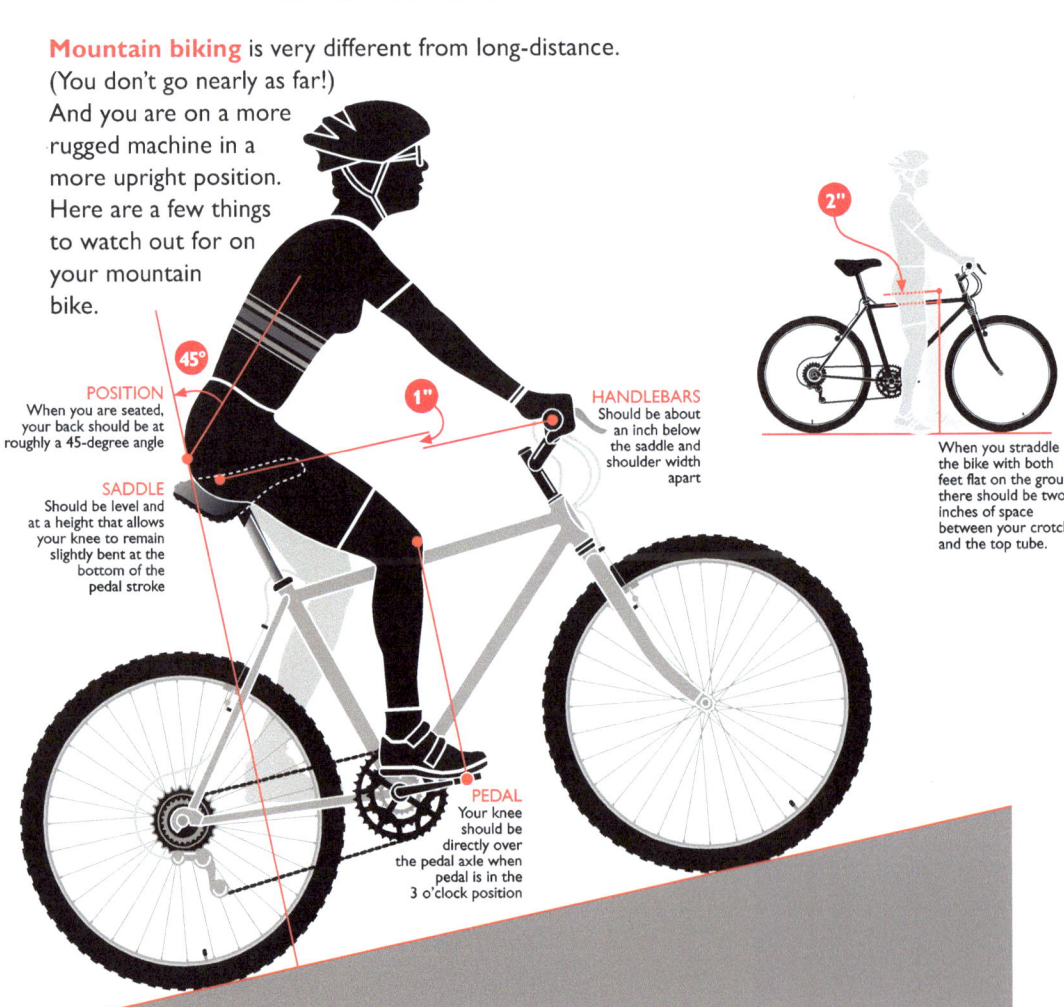

2"

When you straddle the bike with both feet flat on the ground, there should be two inches of space between your crotch and the top tube.

45°

POSITION
When you are seated, your back should be at roughly a 45-degree angle

1"

HANDLEBARS
Should be about an inch below the saddle and shoulder width apart

SADDLE
Should be level and at a height that allows your knee to remain slightly bent at the bottom of the pedal stroke

PEDAL
Your knee should be directly over the pedal axle when pedal is in the 3 o'clock position

Belly dancing

Dancers claim many health benefits of *raks sharki*—the Arabic for *belly dance*. The movements were originally developed to tone your core—glutes, obliques, and quads (→).

Zarafshan Shiraz, writing in the *Hindustan Times* in 2021, cites these benefits:

• Stress relief
Belly dance is likened to a state of meditation from its circular and flowing movements and repetitious swaying.

• Pain relief
The flow of synovial fluid in the lower back and hip joints is enhanced by the gentle and repetitive motions of hip drops and figure-eight movements. Long hours of sitting at work and from our sedentary lifestyle can cause compression of the disks or unnatural curving of the spine. Belly dancing counters this and helps tone back muscles, improving posture.

• It's suitable for all ages
Unlike ballet which can deform the skeleton, belly dancing targets muscle groups in the neck, back, abdomen, and pelvis, which work with the body's physique instead of against it.

• Weight loss
Belly dancing can help you lose weight, as it burns up to 300 calories an hour—depending on the intensity of your dancing.

• PMS relief
Congestion in the pelvic area is alleviated by hip rolling and undulation. The dance moves improve circulation and bring a feeling of relaxation to the pelvic area, keeping PMS woes at bay.

obliques

glutes

quads

Dr. K is skeptical:
Yes, belly dancing is a physical activity, and yes, it has cultural history and significance, and yes, it is entertaining to perform and to watch. But I know of no valid medical research that claims it's fundamentally good for you, or will improve your health. While it does exercise your torso in a special way, a more global approach to strengthening your whole body is better. But go ahead and have fun, as long as you don't conclude that you have exercised your whole body!

Yoga
These are some
of the basic poses
(asanas) with their
common names.

The first thing in a
yoga session is often
The Sun Salutation
sequence

Prayer
pose

Arch
back

Bend
over

Leg
back

Push
up

The
Bridge

The
Bow

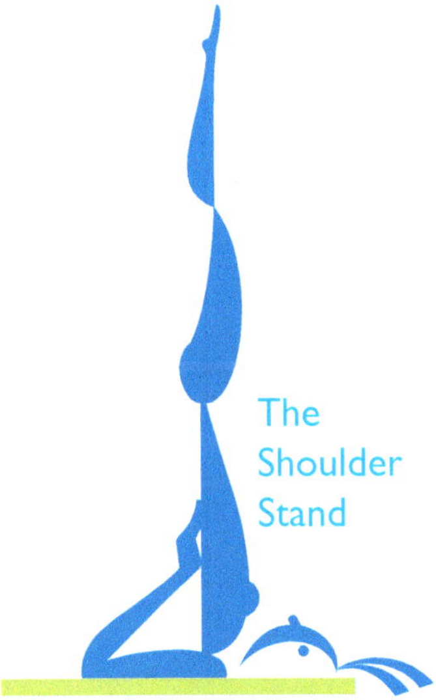

The
Crow

The
Shoulder
Stand

The
Plough

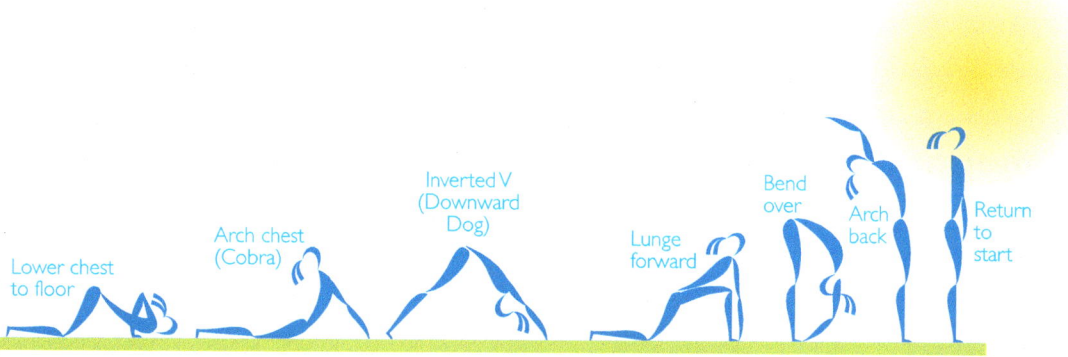

Lower chest to floor

Arch chest (Cobra)

Inverted V (Downward Dog)

Lunge forward

Bend over

Arch back

Return to start

The Triangle

The Tree

The Warrior

Dr. K says:
Yoga makes you more flexible and stronger, without the sweat and six-pack of other exercise programs.

Golf

Since 1552, golf has been played at St Andrews Golf Links, Scotland, where the 18-hole round was established. St Andrews is considered to be the oldest golf course in the world.

Links means the course is built on sandy coastland, and that's why all courses today have bunkers (sand traps) whether or not they are by the sea.)

In **1744**, an early version of the rules of the game was established for a tournament in Edinburgh, Scotland.

In **1899**, St Andrews created a standardized set of rules.

Why do golf balls have dimples?

A typical golf ball has between 300 and 500 dimples creating turbulence in the air around the ball, thus reducing the drag behind it as it wings its way—one hopes—straight to the green.

air
pressure

A smooth ball would fly only about half as far, because the vortex formed behind the ball is stronger, creating a heavy drag.

air
pressure

Keeping the grass green

The amount of water used on golf courses varies depending on their location. Audubon International, a conservation group, estimates a daily average of 312,000 gallons for US courses, but in dryer parts of Arizona and California, it can rise to 1,000,000 gallons *every day*. That's the amount of water a family of four uses in four years.

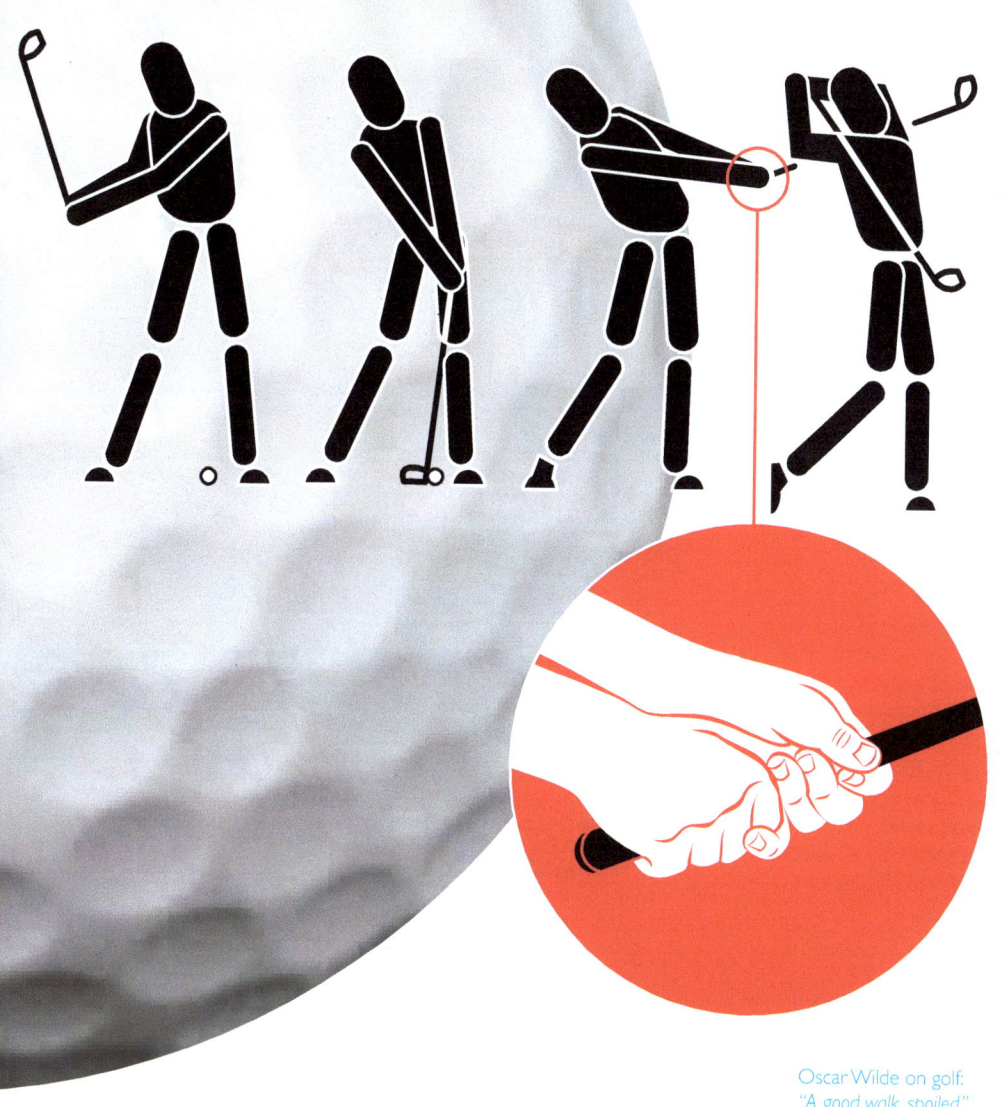

Riding

As a young child, I was lucky enough to be able to ride all sorts of horses at my mother's riding school, in Yorkshire, England. I was small for my age, and whether she was serious or not, my mother told me I was going to be a jockey. Actually, I far preferred to be a cowboy, and even dressed up as one—with a friend who had the same daydreams—when we were allowed to go out riding alone. (My friend had a similarly permissive mother.)

But as much fun as riding like a cowboy was, with a straight leg (→ left), on other occasions (and up to a few years ago) I never rode in the classic "English" style, sitting upright, leg bent at the knee → right). I liked to keep the stirrups shorter than what purists told me was the "right" length. And while my stirrups were never as short as those of a professional jockey (→), something about my mother's jockey career for me lingered on!

As I said a few pages earlier, a lot has been written about the mental health benefits of exercising with animals. Usually, that means walking a dog, but there's scant scientific data to prove this. Riding a horse is different. First you are *on* the animal. You are a team. An emotional bond is formed between the two of you, a bond of trust, on both sides.

True, a horse is more expensive than a dog. In many ways. (A friend likens riding to sailing— which he defines as throwing $100 bills overboard while being soaked to the skin.)

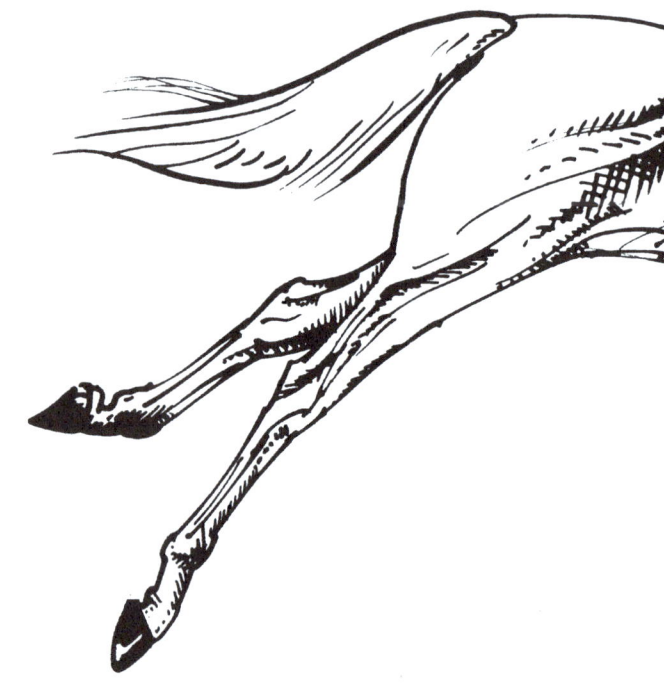

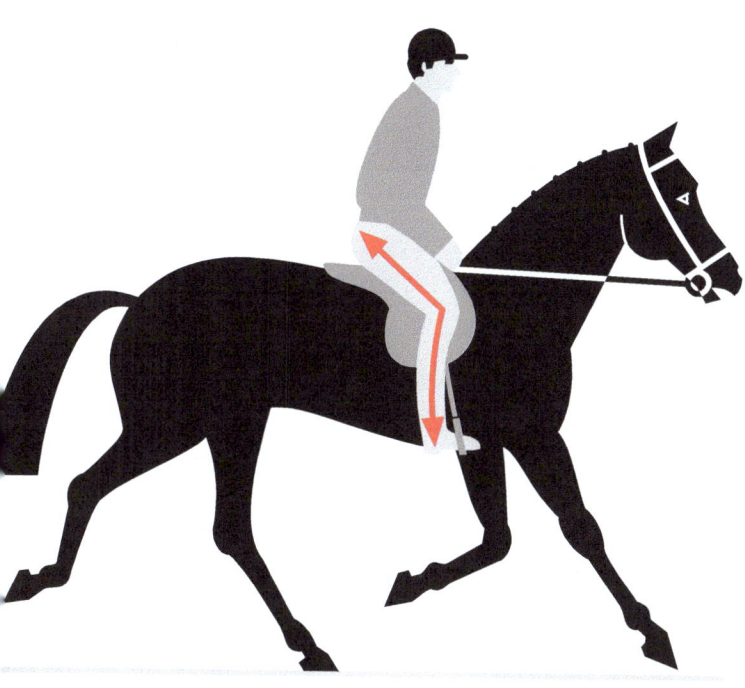

But feeling a huge, strong beast whisk you across an open field is not only exciting, it's romantic (something that I haven't attributed to any other form of exercise!). And it can be dangerous—in the way skiing can be dangerous.

If you ride now, or have in the past, you know what I'm talking about. If not, and someone offers you a ride, go for it! I ♥ horses, and you will too.

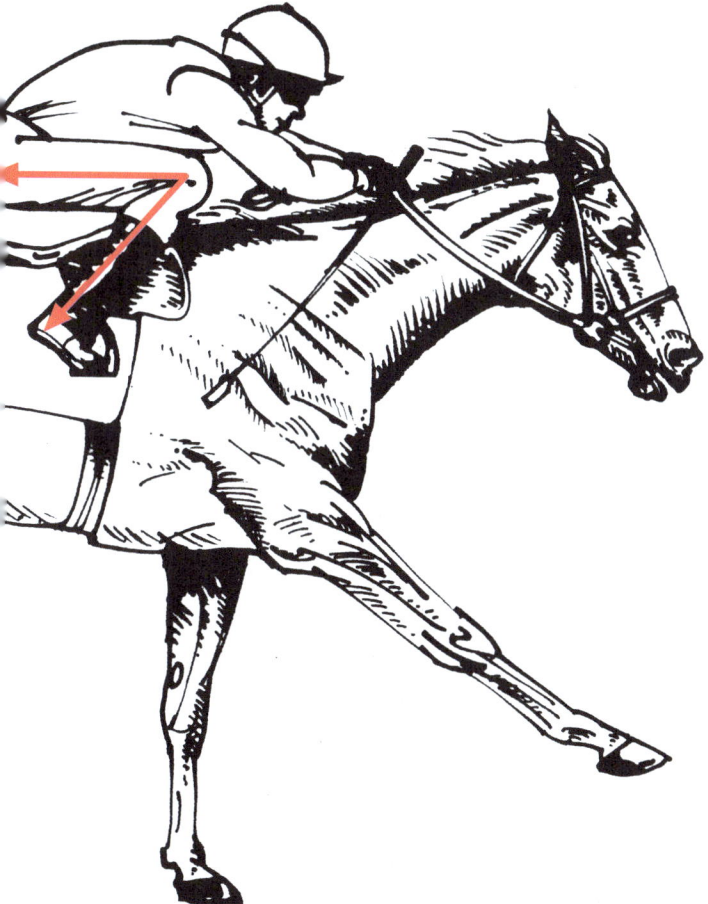

Dr. K says: Jockeys don't weigh much, but it's all muscle. They're strong, but do not use their strength to control the horse, instead using it to stay in perfect balance with their mount, allowing it to move freely and fast. (I used to be an exercise boy at Belmont Racetrack in New York, and years later was the doctor there to the backfield—the invisible part of racing.)

"The outside of a horse is good for the inside of a man," *is a saying that has been variously attributed to Winston Churchill (of course!), Ronald Reagan, and Lord Palmerston, and Dr. K's favorite, Teddy Roosevelt.*

How to twist around four times in the air

You might not be ready for this yourself, but if you skate at all you can still admire a jump that has become an expected part of every Olympic skater's program.

Keys to a successful quad Lutz

- gain height quickly

- start rotating immediately after lift-off

The Quad Lutz is the most difficult jump in figure skating

Moving backwards and to the left, take off from the outside edge of the left skate

A different kind of winter exercise

Like many sports, **speedskating** has taken advantage of technology. If you want to go faster on the ice, it's time to get a pair of **clap skates.** (Looks like you'll need to bulk up those thighs, too.)

You hear a **clap** when the hinged blade snaps back to the boot the moment your foot is lifted off the ice.

spring→

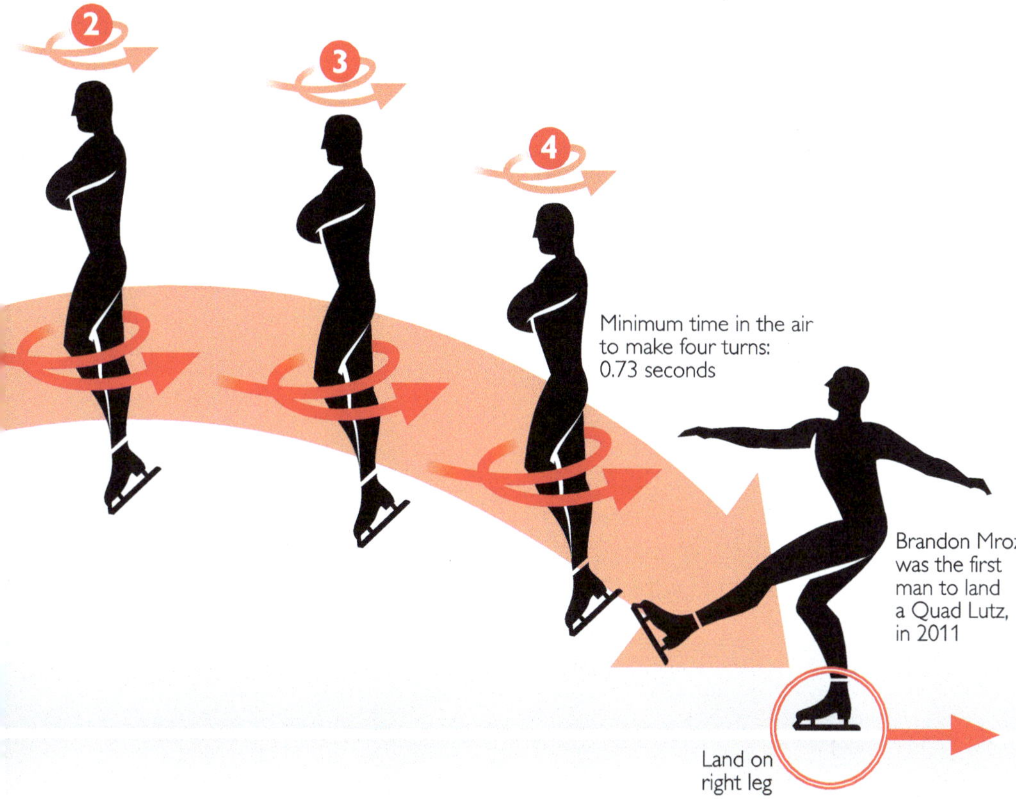

2 **3** **4**

Minimum time in the air to make four turns: 0.73 seconds

Brandon Mroz was the first man to land a Quad Lutz, in 2011

Land on right leg

A **clap skate** allows the edge of a blade to remain in full contact with the ice for an extra moment, even though the boot is beginning to lift off.

The brief added contact with the ice means that you can exert more force on the blade, which in turn generates more speed.

Iichi Marumo is a 95-year-old speedskater from Japan. He competes in races all over the world against other oldsters and invariably wins the gold medal.

Swim tips
Even if you know how to swim, this will improve your form

1 **Kick efficiently: don't let your feet rise above the water line**
This maximises the effort you put into kicking, and minimises drag. (see 2, below.)

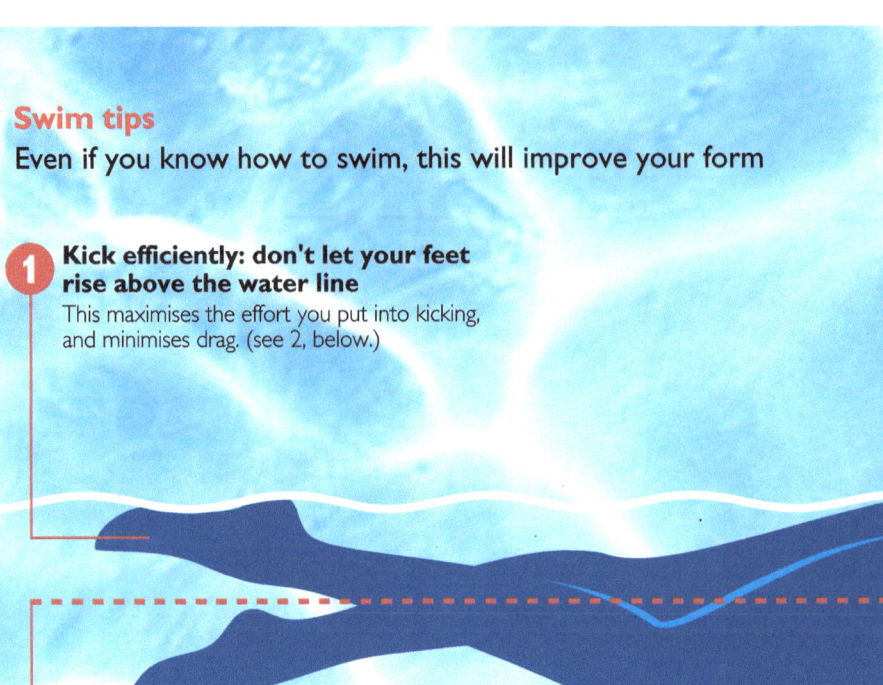

2 **Streamline your body to decrease drag**
You can do this by keeping the body horizontal in the water, and not letting your backside and legs drift downwards. This is called balancing the body.

3 **Instead of swimming on your stomach, roll from side to side with each stroke**
By doing this you'll be presenting a slimmer profile and less resistance to the water, enabling you to glide through it like a fish. And you'll be using the core muscles of your back, hips and torso to apply more force to the stroke.

4 Swim "taller"

Using the principle that a longer, tapered vessel glides through water more easily and faster than a shorter one, reach out as far as you can with each stroke, and leave your hand there longer before retracting to start the next stroke.

5 Keep your head and eyes down

Bringing your head up works against the effort of keeping the body in a straight line—it unbalances you.

6 OK, so you have to breathe!

Raise your head slightly, when you have rolled to one side or the other, to grab a quick breath.

7 Keep your fingers slightly open ...

not tight together nor wide apart. A separation actually makes a web of water between the fingers, giving you more "pull."

Pickle, Paddle, Pádel (and tennis for context)

Pickleball is the most popular net/court sport in America, especially for older people. About 10 million play the game in the US, and there are professional leagues. It's now played in 90+ countries. The sport was invented in 1965 by Joel Pritchard, Bill Bell, and Barney McCallum so they could play a simplified version of tennis—with a solid, short-handled paddle (←), instead of a stringed racquet, and a large, perforated wiffle ball (↓)—in Joel's back yard near Seattle, Washington. The name has nothing to do with pickles: Joel's wife Joan named the sport after "pickle" boats—row boats with crews randomly thrown together, making them the least competitive boats in any race.

Paddle tennis is pickleball's much older cousin. It was created in 1915 by Frank Beal as a children's pastime in the poorer parts of Manhattan, NY. It's like tennis, but played on a smaller court, with a paddle and a regular tennis ball "deadened" by piercing it.

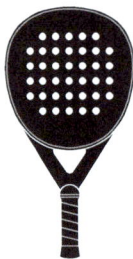

Pádel was invented in 1969 by Enrique Corcuera, in Acapulco, Mexico. It's a doubles game, a blend of squash and tennis, played on artificial turf. You use a perforated paddle (←), and balls that have 75% of the internal pressure of tennis balls. Pádel has about 25 million players worldwide, but its enclosed courts are expensive to build, and clubs with a court charge high fees to play.

How the balls compare (actual size)

Tennis
Paddle tennis
Pádel

Pickleball

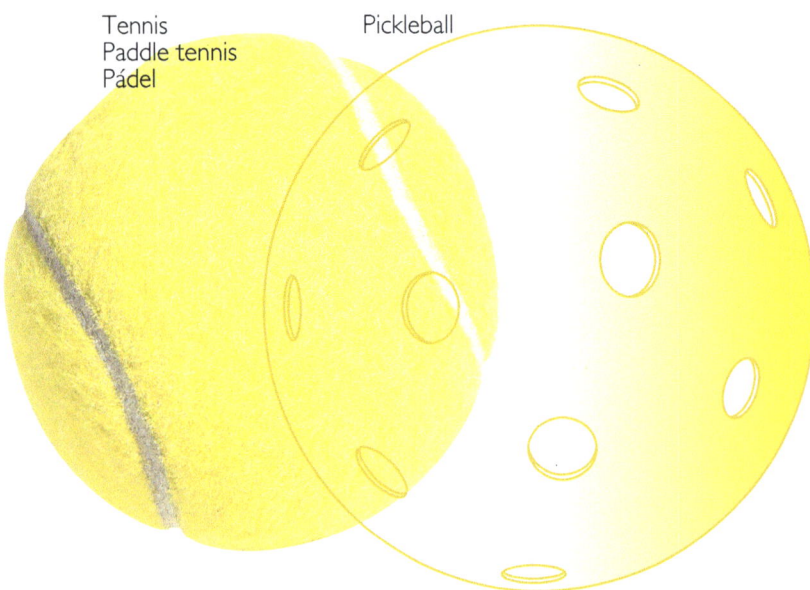

How the courts compare
Pickleball

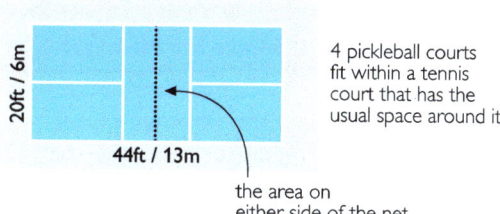

20ft / 6m

44ft / 13m

4 pickleball courts fit within a tennis court that has the usual space around it.

the area on either side of the net is called "the kitchen"

Paddle tennis

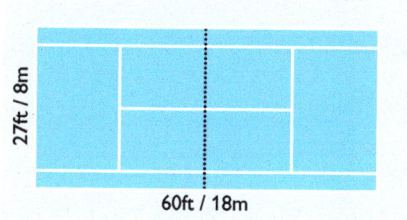

27ft / 8m

60ft / 18m

Pádel

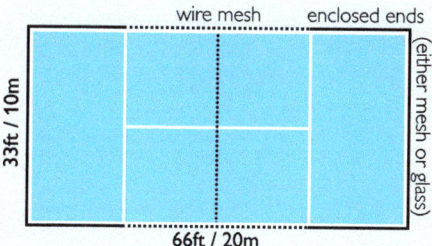

wire mesh   enclosed ends

33ft / 10m

(either mesh or glass)

66ft / 20m

Tiger Woods and Justin Timberlake are part of an investment group that's building a resort in Wellington, Florida, near West Palm Beach. It features 12 pádel courts.

Tennis

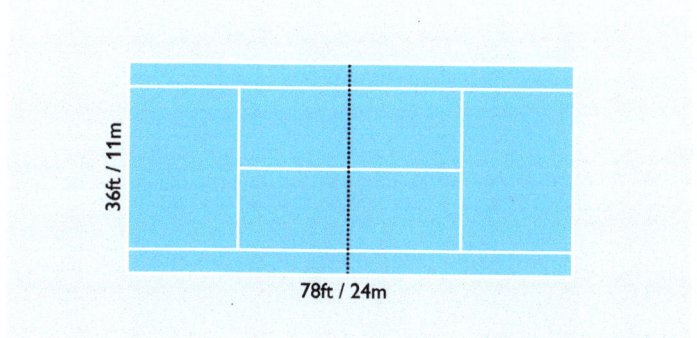

36ft / 11m

78ft / 24m

Two friends kindly replied to my questions about their busy tennis lives.

They play three to four times a week, at different clubs in Santa Barbara, California, but sometimes together as doubles partners if a substitute is needed. Both have an exercise routine that easily matches that of people half their age!

First, *Jan Martin* (←), 91 (in 2025, when we spoke)
When did you start playing tennis? Did you play as a younger person?
I played occasionally in my 30's. In 1973, we joined a tennis club in our neighborhood and I played on weekends mostly because I was working.

Does your club have competitions that you take part in?
I played competitively until seven years ago as a member of the C Team.

How long are your games? Singles or doubles?
We play for one and a half hours, but it's not enforced if the courts are not booked. Always doubles.

Are you competitive? Determined to win?
I think I am competitive—I like to win! However, the exercise factor is very important to me!

What's your best stroke?
I think my best and favorite stroke is my two-handed backhand.

Do you stretch before or after playing?
Unfortunately, I am not disciplined about solitary exercises, so I rarely stretch.

Any other exercises, not related to tennis?
I try to do a 3- to 4-mile walk at least once a week.

Do you feel good after playing?
I am happy and pleased that I am able to do this weekly exercise.

Do you play on a hard court, or clay, or grass?
I play on hard court at the club and at our municipal courts. I have played on clay occasionally. It's interesting that my knees are not as problematic as they were six months ago. No issues recently!

Any other injuries?
About 20 or so years I fell on the court chasing down a ball and ruptured an Achilles tendon and broke a wrist. Occasionally, arthritis flare-ups will create some discomfort.

Do you have a favorite player?
I saw Jannik Sinner play at Indian Wells last March and I've become a fan. (I am aware of the doping controversy.)

And this (←) is *Nancy Pierson*, 89 (in 2025)

When did you start playing tennis? Did you play as a younger person?
If hitting the ball against a chimney counts, yes, and then a little in high school. No lessons, just hit the ball and get it over the net. I was fast and furious and played for fun. Jan and I played with our husbands a few times and I played with a neighborhood group. About 24 years ago, I took it up again. I had stopped running, needed an exercise and have been playing ever since.

How long are your games?
Each session is two hours with a chat here and there.

Do you play singles and/or doubles?
Doubles, with ladies 65 and up (mostly up).

Are you competitive? Determined to win?
Not competitive, but I play to keep the ball away from my opponent—I play for fun and exercise.

What's your best stroke?
Whatever gets it over the net!

Do you stretch before or after playing?
No, I know I should.

Any other exercises, not related to tennis?
I do Pilates twice a week and I walk 3-4 miles on Saturdays.

Do you feel good afterward?
Sometimes the lungs get in the way; or my eye (the bad one) gets clouded over and I don't like to let my partner down when we lose. Otherwise, I feel great, fortunate to play and socialize.

Is there some sort of reward afterward?
My reward is being able to still play.

Do you have a favorite player?
Federer, Nadal; mostly the ones who are not arrogant and angry.

A couple of eccentric physical activities to enliven the office lunch hour, or holiday party. (Probably best to do both of these outdoors.)

You can't make this stuff up—these are actual events.

The annual **World Mobile Phone Throwing Championships** are held in Savonlinna, Finland, in late August.

Contestants throw original phones, with batteries. They are provided by the organizers.

There are four categories of competition, including one for kids 12 years old and younger, and team events.

World records
(as of 2019)
Men: 362.3 ft (110.4 m)
Women: 226.6 ft (67.6 m)

Other countries that have phone-throwing competitions:
Belgium
Canada
Czech Republic
India
Liechtenstein
Norway
Spain
UK

What happens to the phones?

The event was started in 2000 by Nokia as a way to **recycle** them. Instead of being recycled, phones were thrown into lakes in Finland, where their batteries became toxic waste.

The World Championships is doing its bit to stop toxic elements from polluting the air and water.

Office Chair Racing was an event in Bad König, Germany for some years, until a shopping arcade in Kyotanabe, Kyoto, Japan used the idea as a marketing stunt, and called it the **ISU-1 Grand Prix.** (Isu = chair in Japanese.) **Office chair racing is now popular in many parts of Japan.**

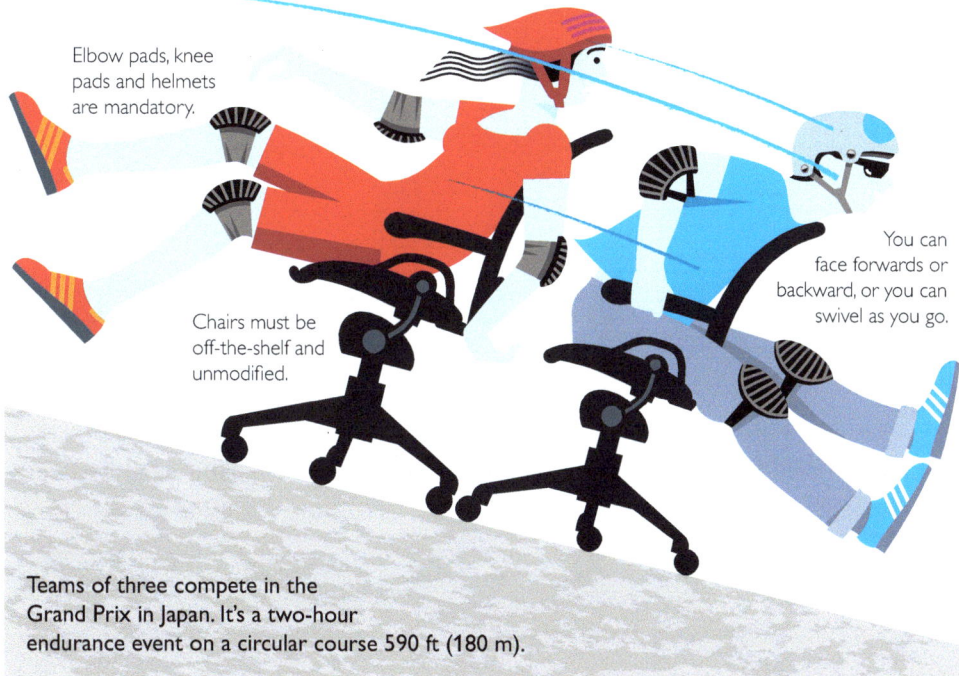

Elbow pads, knee pads and helmets are mandatory.

You can face forwards or backward, or you can swivel as you go.

Chairs must be off-the-shelf and unmodified.

Teams of three compete in the Grand Prix in Japan. It's a two-hour endurance event on a circular course 590 ft (180 m).

And here are three sports for people with tons of money!

Real tennis ("Court" tennis in the US) originated in the 16th century in England, and was played by English and French nobility, fully dressed in silks and wigs. It's a cross between squash and regular tennis. Today, it has found a small but devoted following with a total of about 45 active courts in the UK, France, Australia, and the US. The asymmetric court is complex and *very* expensive for clubs to build, so the whole thing is a pretty exclusive affair.

The court (↓) has markings (and rules) that sound like a satirical take on insider jargon (see: "1 Yard Worse Than Last"), and the rules themselves are so complicated that videos I watched were barely able to explain them. For instance, an earnest description of how the second bounce of a ball in any play "*leads to a 'chase,' which then has to be 'called out,' with neither player getting a point at that time—but which then has to be played again at the end of the game*"—had me totally confused.

The "Penthouses" (←) are one-story constructions within the court area with slanted roofs—which are part of the playing area.

If you ever can fully understand the rules, real tennis does look like good exercise!

Real tennis equipment is as eccentric as the rest of the game. Racquets (a nod to the way they are spelled in England) are 27in (68mm) long, smaller than their regular tennis counterparts, and feature this jaunty angle (↓).

Real tennis balls are harder and heavier than regular tennis balls. They have a cork core wrapped tightly with twine and covered with cloth.

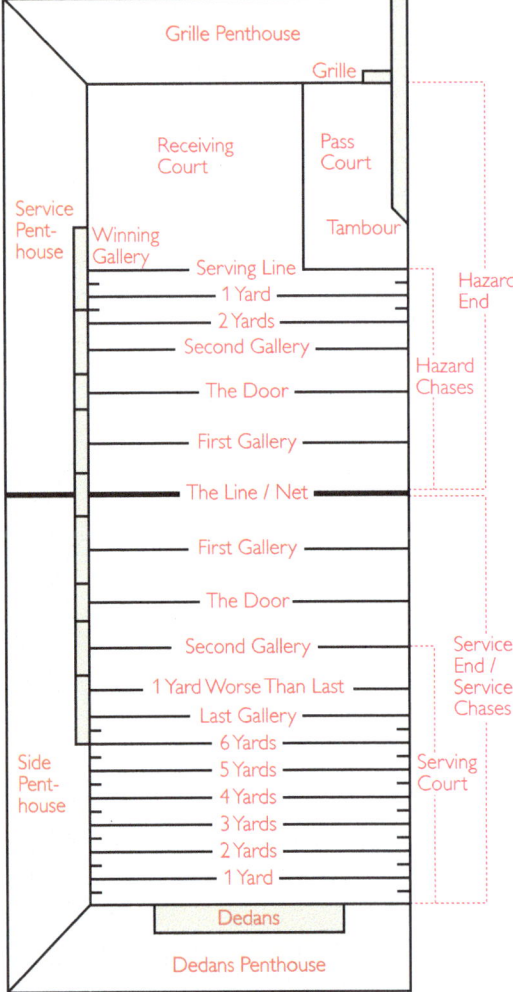

Beagling is a form of hunting with dogs that's like fox hunting—beagles are similar to foxhounds, just smaller. Hunters wear a green traditional costume (←), but unlike fox hunting (where hunters wear red (→) and ride horses), beaglers run on the ground after the hounds. Their prey is rabbits or hares. The "sport" is governed in England by the Hunting Act of 2004, which allows it if the animal being "flushed out" would seriously damage crops or if it's going to be eaten.

The outfit you see on Ye Olde English Prints. Usually only the Masters of the Hunt wear red, others wear black jackets.

The Cresta Run in St. Moritz, Switzerland, is a one-minute slide on a minuscule sled or toboggan (called a skeleton) down a three-quarter mile ice run (↓), head first, reaching 90mph (145kph) at the bottom. Many injuries. The run is built from scratch every year, and is open from just before Christmas to the end of February.

The Cresta Run was used for skeleton events at the 1928 and 1948 Winter Olympics. (Skeleton became a permanent Olympic event in 2002.)

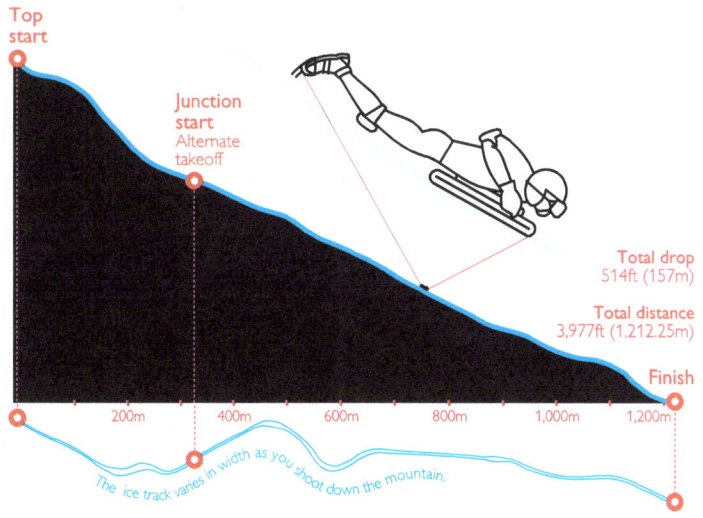

Top start

Junction start
Alternate takeoff

Total drop
514ft (157m)

Total distance
3,977ft (1,212.25m)

Finish

200m 400m 600m 800m 1,000m 1,200m

The ice track varies in width as you shoot down the mountain.

The St. Moritz Tobogganing Club Ltd is a private organization of amateur riders whose members are elected from a "Supplementary List." To get on the list, beginners must book a three-run practice session with a club guru, after which they are called SL members.

Once you are on the Supplementary List, it costs 500 CHF (Swiss Francs) for five rides. The fee includes a helmet, boots with rakes (for braking and steering), handguards, elbow and knee pads, and a toboggan.

If you don't like the gym, or any of the exercises you've seen here so far, don't worry, you may be getting fit, anyway!

Do you dance?

Do you carry your kid?

Do you dig?

CATS RULE

MEOW

Do you march?

Do you push?

Do you shovel?

Do you take things upstairs?

Do you dust?

Do you drum?

Do you bend over?

AND REMEMBER...→

YOU
DON'T
HAVE TO
EXCERCISE
EVERY DAY.

YOUR BODY
LOVES IT
WHEN
YOU
ALLOW
IT TO
REST
AND YOU
JUST
DREAM

SIX 6

Three-Rep

Dr. Kasofsky's fast, easy, at-home exercises.

Dr. K. says: The whole Three-Rep program should take you no more than 8–12 minutes; see if you can do it at least three times a week. For the first group of exercises, you are standing up. Later, you are on the floor.

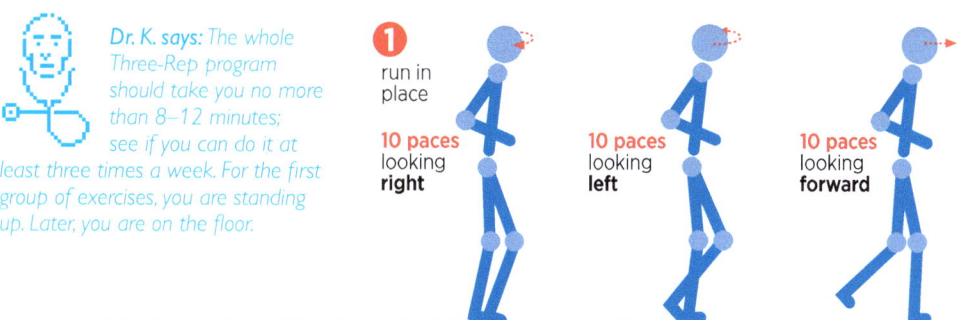

1

run in place

10 paces looking **right**

10 paces looking **left**

10 paces looking **forward**

You noticed! The very first exercise doesn't have 3 reps. Most of the others do.

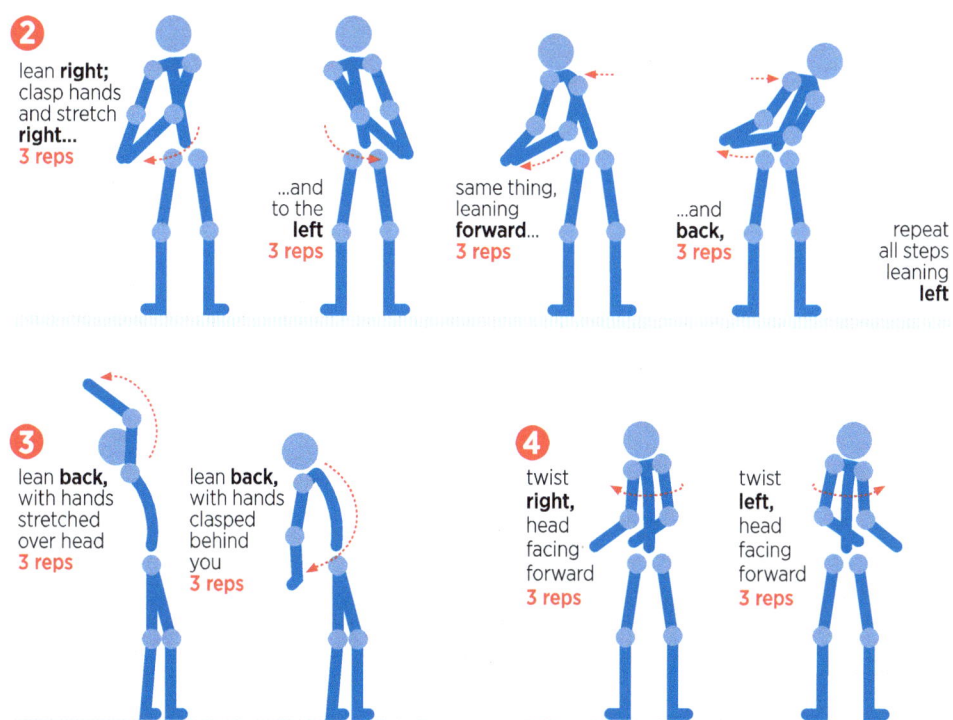

2

lean **right;** clasp hands and stretch **right...**
3 reps

...and to the **left**
3 reps

same thing, leaning **forward...**
3 reps

...and **back,**
3 reps

repeat all steps leaning **left**

3

lean **back,** with hands stretched over head
3 reps

lean **back,** with hands clasped behind you
3 reps

4

twist **right,** head facing forward
3 reps

twist **left,** head facing forward
3 reps

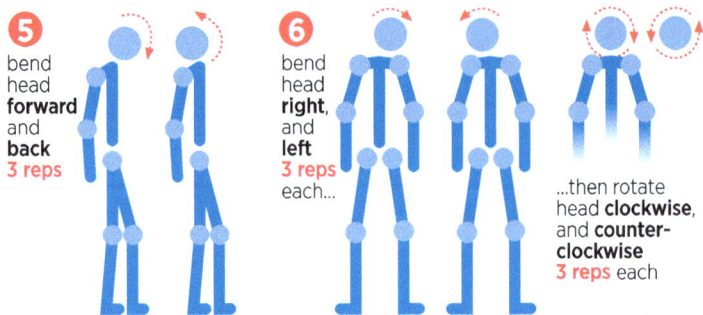

⑤ bend head **forward** and **back** 3 reps

⑥ bend head **right**, and **left** 3 reps each...

...then rotate head **clockwise**, and **counter-clockwise** 3 reps each

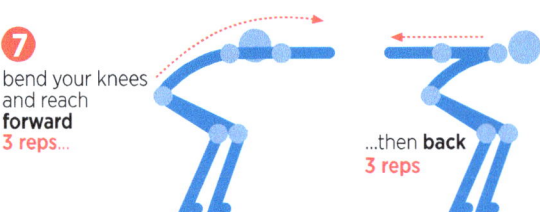

⑦ bend your knees and reach **forward** 3 reps...

...then **back** 3 reps

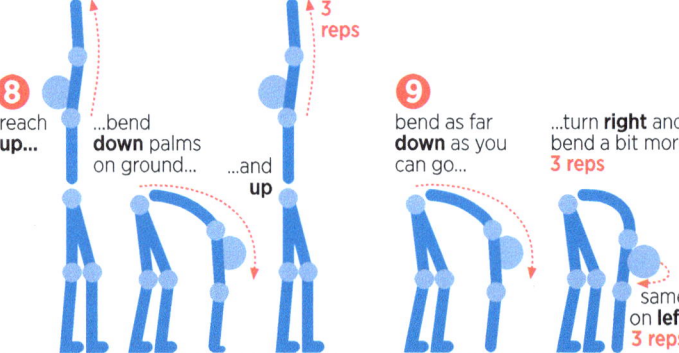

⑧ reach **up**... ...bend **down** palms on ground... ...and **up** 3 reps

⑨ bend as far **down** as you can go... ...turn **right** and bend a bit more 3 reps

same on **left** 3 reps

stay down, let body relax, go further

Dr. K reminds us: All exercise programs advise a consultation with a doctor before starting.

Successful programs achieve results by changing people's movements, building muscle mass, and elongating ligaments, and by strengthening your tendons, skeletal articulation, bone mass, and internal bone structure.

Three-Rep is a gentler, more gradual and less demanding program than others, achieving results by subtly, kindly, altering your body's configuration. (But you should still see a doctor before starting.)

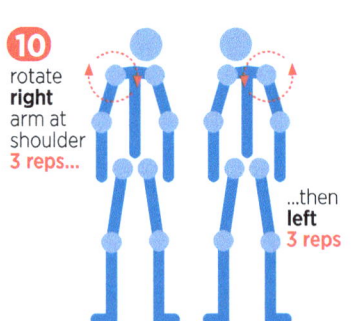

⑩ rotate **right** arm at shoulder 3 reps...

...then **left** 3 reps

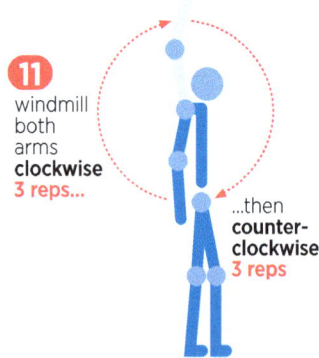

⑪ windmill both arms **clockwise** 3 reps...

...then **counter-clockwise** 3 reps

12
bend arms
at elbows
reach
forward
3 reps...

...and
back
3 reps

*Exercise 12 is good for
preventing and even healing
a torn rotator cuff.
(It could save you a trip to
an orthopedic surgeon.)*

13
get your
balance
and kick
right
with
right
leg,
3 reps

14
With
knee
bent,
lift thigh
3 reps...

...then
repeat
on **left**
3 reps

no touching the floor!

15
knee
bends
3 reps

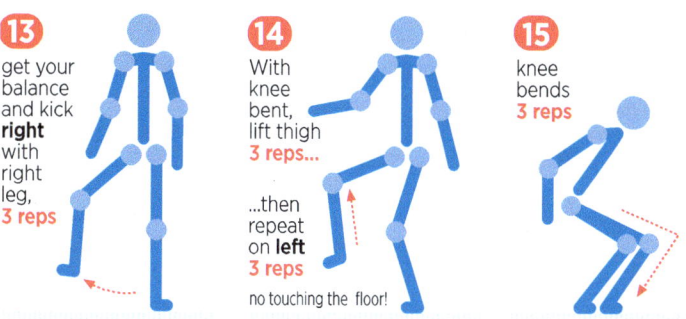

16
stand 2-3 feet from the
bed; lean over; hold the
frame; stretch as far
as possible **3 reps...**

...then stretch **left 3 reps;** and **right 3 reps**

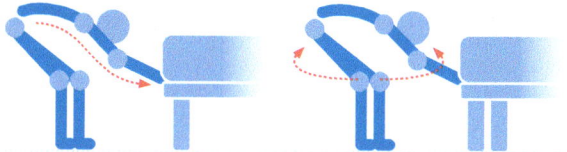

17
stand on
your **left**
foot and
lift the
right one
a little bit
for **10
seconds...**

...repeat,
standing on
right foot
10 seconds

first, with eyes open, then a round with eyes closed

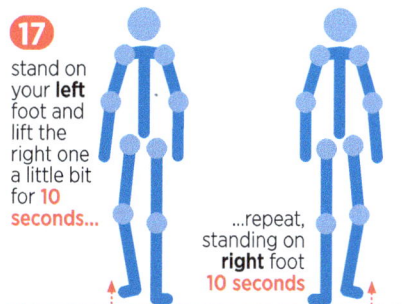

18
from a
standing
position,
squat
3 reps

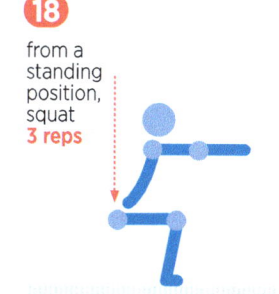

*A slight variation: make the
last rep of each group of
three a few seconds longer,
with an extra stretch or
reach—a minimal, left-right,
side-to-side rotation.*

Time taken so far:
about **3 minutes.**

19 on back, raise both legs at the same time **3 reps...** ...then twist feet right and left **3 reps**

20 lift both hips up **3 reps**

21 bend **right** knee, hold, **3 reps** same with **left, 3** cross **right** foot over and hold with left hand, **3 reps...** ...same with **left** foot, **3 reps**

22 lie on left side, lift **right** leg, **3 reps...** ...then raise leg **3 reps** ...rotate leg **clockwise 3 reps...** ...then **counter-clockwise 3 reps** repeat all, lying on right side

Splits are hard! Slowly, gently just do what you can.

23 splits: **right** leg forward **3 reps,** then **left 3 reps**

24 push ups: **low 3 reps**

25 push ups: **deeper 3 reps**

26 plank: **hold** for **10 seconds**

Exercise 27: at first, you might like to support your back with your hands as you curl up.

27 **curl** body, move butt toward head... ...then **uncurl** toward legs **3 reps**

28 rest buttocks on heels **hold** for **3 seconds...** ...then twist **right** and **left 3 reps** each

29
bend knees,
stretch **forward**
3 reps

30
with straight legs
spread open,
lift up 6 inches,
close together, open again
3 reps

31
bicycle
3 reps
forwards...

...**3 reps**
backwards

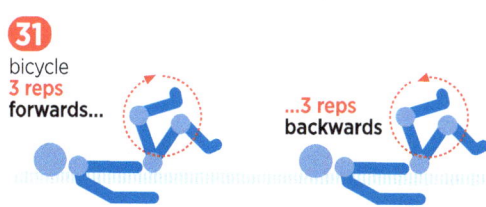

*No pain, no gain?
It's unfortunately correct, but
there is NO need to overdo
the pain. A little ache, a bit of
tightness? It happens when
exercising. Try a heating pad.
Do it lightly next time. Skip a
day or two. Allowing muscles,
ligaments and tendons to
have some intervals of rest
helps them grow and adapt
better.*

32
sit ups
3 reps
forward...

...**3 reps**
to the
right...

...**3 reps**
to the
left

33
bend knees,
sit up,
**elbows to
kneecaps**
3 reps

press knees,
inwards,
hold for
3 seconds
3 reps

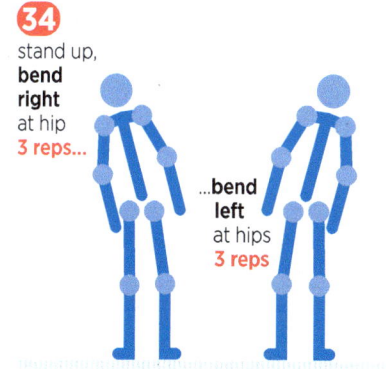

side view   front view

34
stand up,
**bend
right**
at hip
3 reps...

...**bend
left**
at hips
3 reps

35
**bend
forward,**
put palms on the ground,
up and down
3 reps

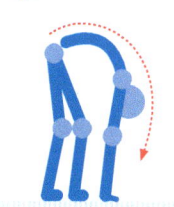

*Many of Japan's corporations
have a pause in the day
for employees to do a brief
stretching and exercise
routine. Short, and much
like the Three-Rep program,
it's designed for the whole
body, and is intended to
keep the workforce fit—and
presumably able to work
longer hours!*

You're done!
Total time taken:
about **8-12 minutes.**

*Lie flat on your back on the
floor in "corpse" pose,
(Shavasana in yoga) for 3–5
minutes. A cup of tea, perhaps?*

Dr. K says: If you stick with the Three-Rep program you
won't have a six-pack, and you
won't have marked definition, and you
won't win any competition at the gym—because you
won't need to go there!

But you will...

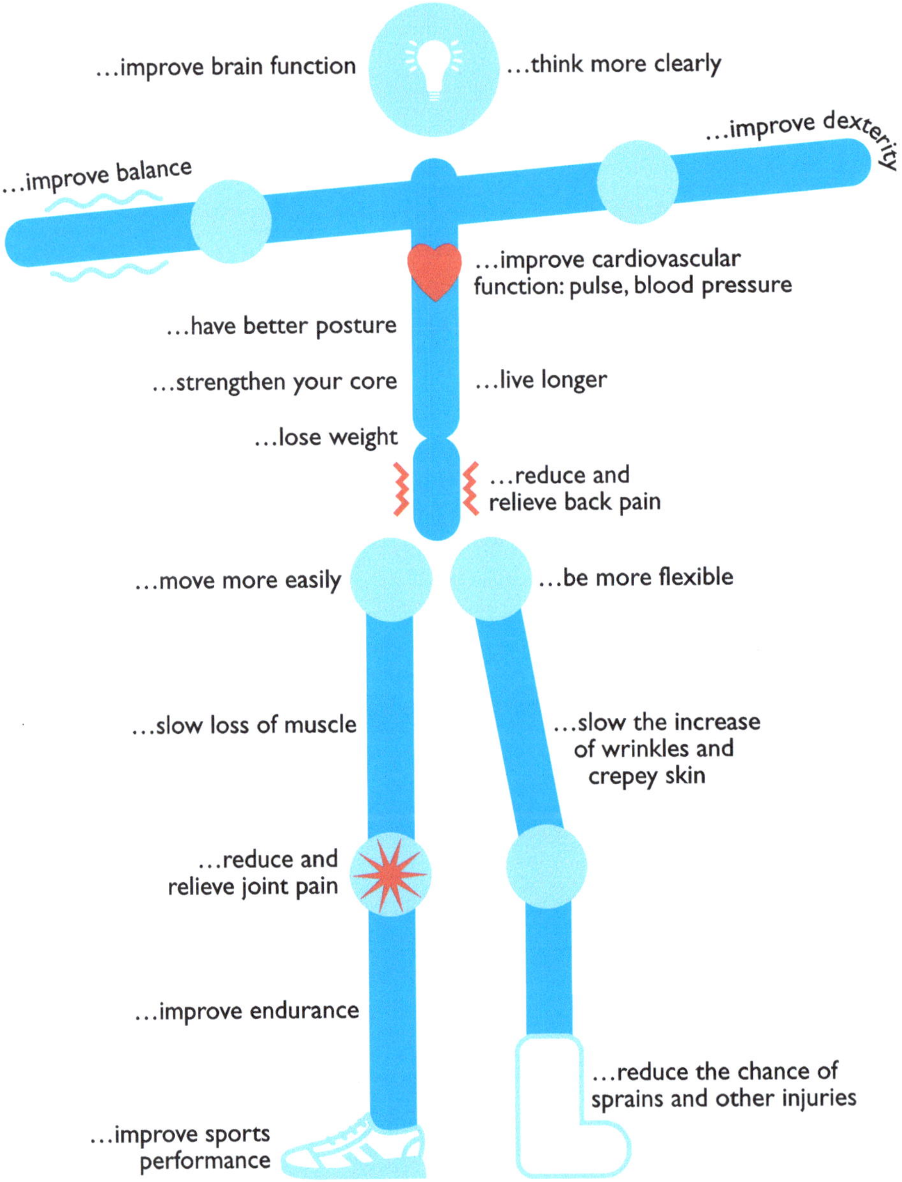

...improve brain function

...think more clearly

...improve dexterity

...improve balance

...improve cardiovascular function: pulse, blood pressure

...have better posture

...strengthen your core

...live longer

...lose weight

...reduce and relieve back pain

...move more easily

...be more flexible

...slow loss of muscle

...slow the increase of wrinkles and crepey skin

...reduce and relieve joint pain

...improve endurance

...reduce the chance of sprains and other injuries

...improve sports performance

You can modify the routine, but please remember the spirit of Three-Rep is simplicity, brevity, sustainability, semi-regularity, fun, and ease. If you do feel like going just a bit further, or want to improve your posture and flexibility, here are three enhancements:

1
20 sit-ups
3–4 times a week before going to bed—or *in* bed. You'll be alert enough to read in bed for 30+ minutes, then you'll sleep deeper, longer. . . .

It's best to do the sit-ups at a different time from the program itself.
(I do the Three-Rep routine in the morning.)

2
Wear weights
on your wrists and ankles as you exercise; 2–5lb (1–2.5kg) are enough to build more muscle and increase your stretching without overdoing things.

Additional time required: one minute to put the weights on (and off).

3
Hang upside down.
Gravity can do bad things to your back. So reverse the effects by hanging upside down. It's good for posture, back pain, back movement. You can hang with gravity boots, or by using an inversion table (↓), fitted with a device to secure your feet so you don't need gravity boots.

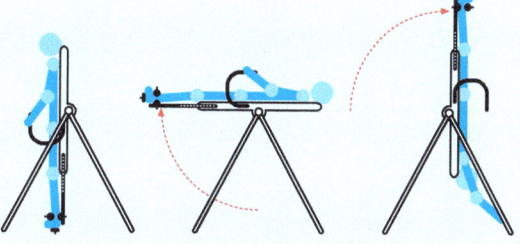

Long ago, I hurt my back (probably a disk problem). Saw an ad for gravity boots, tried them and was riding again two weeks later. Never looked back. I'm a believer. Now I do it 2–3 times a week.

Being upside down is a bit unpleasant at first; the blood seems to pool in your head and the sensation of pressure building is not fun. After a while, you figure out the right clothing (no neck constriction, such as a turtle-neck sweater), the correct angle not to impede jugular vein flow, and importantly, the right breathing pattern—just a bit deeper than usual.

I can now bend right and left and do partial sit-ups against gravity. Sometimes I hold 10- or 20lb weights.

SEVEN

OW!!

What could possibly go wrong?
Sprains and strains and tears and fractures and pain, that's what!

Dr. K says:
As an emergency room doctor,
I see all kinds of injuries,
from minor to major.

Let's start with some definitions:
A sprain *is a pulled ligament or tendon. (Ligaments are bands of tissue that connect to bones, in a joint.) The most common occurrence of this kind of injury is ankles.*

A strain *is a pulled muscle or tendon. (Tendons are bands of tissue that connect muscles to bones.) Most common occurrence: hamstrings and lower back.*

A tear (or rupture) *can be a ligament, tendon, muscle, or skin.*

A fracture, *that's a bone.*

Four ways to tell which are serious and which are less so:

1. *Is there a lot of* **pain***?*
Pain is the body's way of telling you something is wrong.
For a sprain, there will be pain, bruising,
and swelling around the affected joint.
For a strain, there will be pain spasms,
and swelling around the affected area.

2. *What are the* **mechanics** *of the accident?*
If you fell 30 feet—that's a serious injury, unless you're lucky. A 3lb weight fell on your toe in the gym—not much. A high speed rollover in your car—serious! A 5mph bump—not much.

3. Appearance.
If there's deformity, it's possibly a fracture, but if it looks good, the odds are there isn't a fracture. (Same goes for swelling or ecchymosis—the doctor's fancy word for "black and blue.")

Dr. K: I'm one of the old guard of ER doctors, and I have noticed that Americans' level of pain perception has increased enormously, while their ability to endure it has decreased. The doctor (James Campbell of the American Pain Society) who called pain the "Fifth Vital Sign," in 1996, where patients rated their pain level from 1 to 10, has regretted the whole idea. Pain perception and endurance are a cultural thing and ours has moved radically to the wimpy side. No one ever tells me their pain is a 3; they say it's a 12, way off the scale.

4. Tenderness.

Not so easy to tell what happened, but if there is extreme tenderness in one spot, I would suspect a fracture.

So, what do doctors do in these different cases?

X-rays, CT scans, MRIs, radioactive imaging. One of those usually settles the issue. If the bones are shown to be OK, then it's a strain or a fracture. If the bones are in pieces...well, you get the picture (literally!)

Years ago doctors thought we could tell fractures from sprains by simply examining the injured part, using "clinical judgment." That's wrong, and leads to surprises. Personally, I x-ray just about everything. I'm still surprised by what I see, or don't see.

Back problems:

Evolution didn't get everything right—like backs. We evolved to move. But today we are often sedentary; we move less (and gain weight). Motion keeps our backs in shape, and not doing much leads to muscle and bone loss. I might see a 97-year-old with a perfect cardiogram. I never see a 97-year-old with a perfect back x-ray.

Greenland sharks are the world's longest living vertebrates, largely due to their extremely slow rate of metabolism.

They grow up to 23 feet, and weigh 1.5 tons. (As a comparison, Great White sharks reach about 15 feet, but weigh 2.5 tons.)

Sharks are designed a lot better. A recently discovered Greenland shark is thought to be over 400 years old. We humans get disabling disk disease, arthritis, loss of strength from low calcium (osteoporosis), and fractures, with reduced movement and pain. Greenland sharks are still swimming when they are 400 years old!

Backs need a redesign! But that won't happen, so we need to know how to take better care of them. Try these simple exercises (→).

You can do them at home, but as with all exercises, go gently at first. If you continue the moves regularly (even when the pain has subsided), you'll strengthen your back muscles, and there'll be less chance anything will happen next time you pick up a heavy box, and your back doesn't like it.

*And try the **Three-Rep** routine (see Chapter 6, especially exercise number 9) to strengthen your core—abdomen, the side and back muscles of your torso—maintaining flexibility and range of motion.*

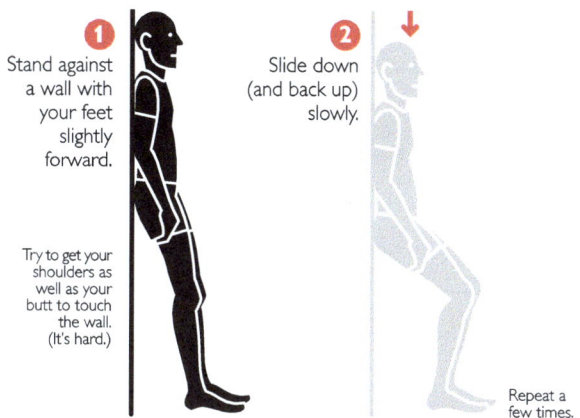

1 Stand against a wall with your feet slightly forward.

Try to get your shoulders as well as your butt to touch the wall. (It's hard.)

2 Slide down (and back up) slowly.

Repeat a few times.

1 Sit up straight.

2 Reach as far as you can.

1 Kneel on floor.

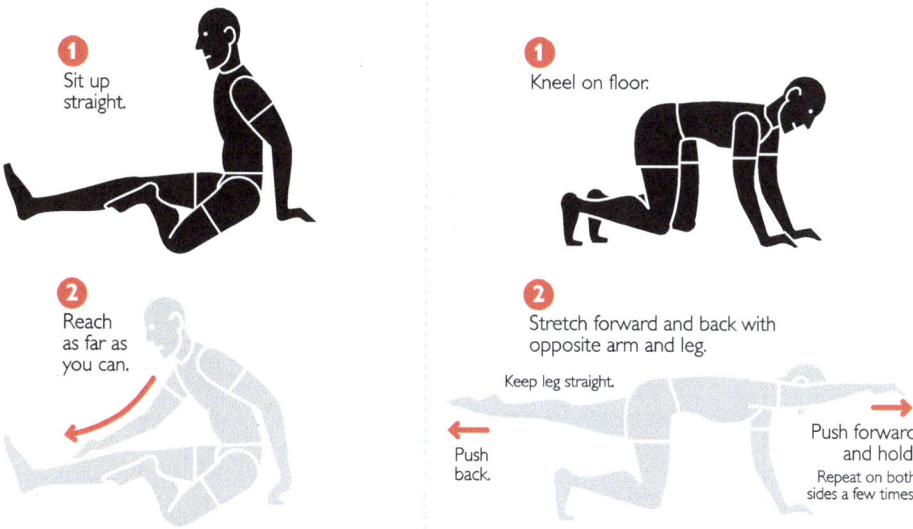

2 Stretch forward and back with opposite arm and leg.

Keep leg straight.

Push back.

Push forward and hold.

Repeat on both sides a few times.

1 Lie on your back with knees bent; raise torso.

2 Bring knee to opposite elbow.

Repeat on both sides, in a continuous back-and-forth flow.

Pointed toes do not touch floor.

1 Lie flat on your tummy.

2 Raise whole body to "plank" position off the floor. Hold for a few seconds and repeat.

Keep legs straight.

Bad accidents happen, but you can help. CPR is the emergency treatment that's done when someone is not breathing, or is taking gasping breaths, or when their heart has stopped beating.

How to do CPR:

Cardio-
Pulmonary   = reviving the
Resuscitation   heart and lungs

1 **Call emergency services.**

2 If the victim is not breathing normally, nor coughing or moving, **start chest pumping.**

↓

Push down, in the centre of the chest **5cm (2in), 30 times.**

3 Keep going **hard and fast.** You should be pumping at least **100 times a minute,** faster than once a second.

This might seem like a lot. You may actually break ribs doing it.

4 **Continue** until there are signs of movement, or until emergency medical personnel take over.

5cm (2in)

5 Continuous, hard **chest pumping** is considered to be the most important part of CPR.

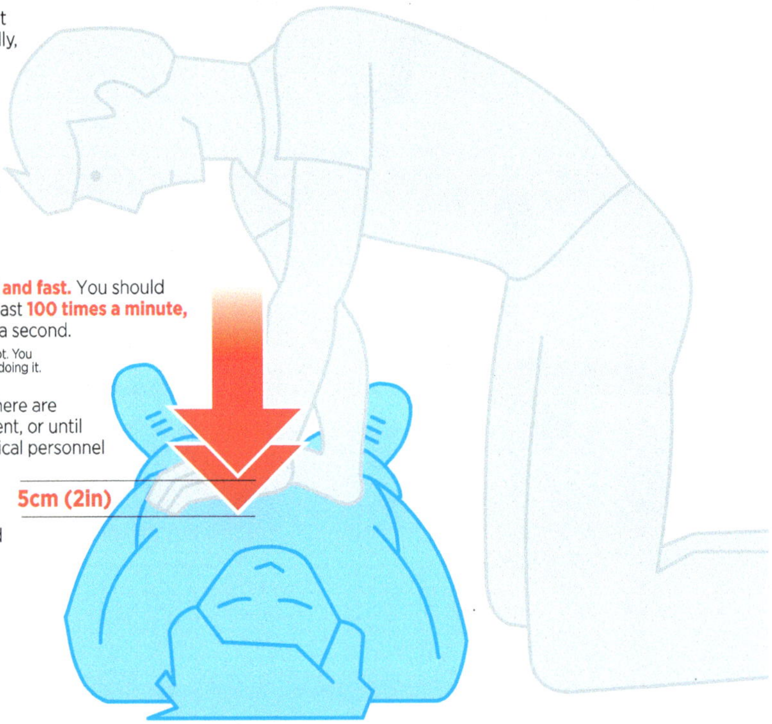

Mouth-to-mouth? Many people don't engage in mouth-to-mouth resuscitation for for fear of disease, or because they are squeamish about doing it. In fact, it's highly unlikely that you will get a disease, and filling the lungs with air is important, so here's what you do:

1 **Tilt the victim's head back** and listen for possible sounds of coughing or vomiting. (One result of pumping the chest is that the victim vomits. Turn the head to the side, and try to wipe the liquid out of the way.)

2 Pinch the nose and cover the mouth with yours. **Blow** in until you see the chest rise. Do this **twice.**

3 **Repeat 30 pumps and two breaths** until help comes.

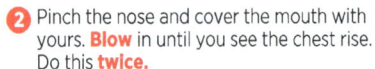

4 Two people giving CPR is good: one pumping, one blowing air in. (Take turns, do not do both at once.)

Dr. K. says:

CPR is integral to and an important part of current medical treatment. Everyone should know how to do it, and do it correctly. The sooner CPR is done, the sooner a heart patient is appropriately shocked by an AED (automated external defibrillator), the better the results.

But reality has a way of upsetting the glossy view of CPR, and the reality is that a low percentage of people with heart attacks, life-threatening heart rhythms, and severe respiratory problems are actually saved by CPR.

The numbers are pretty grim: immediate CPR and shocking of a patient who has cardiac arrest while in hospital produces the best results—13% leave the hospital and live for 12 months.

Outside the hospital, even if a team of trained paramedics does the job, the equivalent success rate is 7%.

In the ER, even if we know it will probably be useless, we do it anyway, usually exceeding the guidelines of the American College of Cardiology, who establish and improve CPR guidelines.

The Automated External Defibrillator

If a person appears to have had a heart attack, or has problems breathing, call for emergency help.

These instructions are from the Mayo Clinic, NY.

CPR (←) can be started while you prepare the AED.

When you turn on the machine, it gives you step-by-step voice instructions—how to check for breathing and a pulse, and how and where to place the AED pads on the person's bare chest.

After putting the pads in place, do not touch the person while the AED measures the heartbeat.

If the machine senses that a shock is needed, it will tell the user to stand back and push a button to deliver the shock.

Make sure no one (including yourself) is touching the person. Loudly announce "Stand clear," and push the shock button.

The universal AED sign was developed by the International Liaison Committee on Resuscitation. (It's often printed

After this, continue CPR, until professional help arrives.

Replace the batteries regularly. Some machines have built-in alarms to remind you. Just make sure the machine is in a place where you can hear the alarm.

in red in the US.)

Sativa

Indica

Dr. K. says:
I'm starting to see increased numbers of patients in the emergency room with weed overuse symptoms—largely intestinal, vomiting, and psychiatric. Be careful.

Cannabis is not considered an athletic performance enhancer. But to calm their nerves, athletes could use it at the proposed **Enhanced Games,** the brainchild of Aron D'Souza—an idea facing considerable opposition from the International Olympic Committee and the World Anti-Doping Agency. As of 2025, no host city, or cities have been chosen. The plan is for different events to be held in separate cities and at different times of the year. At his *Enhanced Games,* Mr. D'Souza thinks that it may be possible for an "enhanced" 65-year-old to "run faster than the fastest *natural* human."

Can cannabis help if you are injured?

Ultimately, this comes down to personal choice, because the products made from the two prevalent weed plants, *Sativa* and *Indica*, affect people differently. *Sativa* has a higher ratio of THC (tetrahydrocannabinol) to CBD (cannabidiol); *Indica* has the opposite ratio—more CBD than THC.

THC is what gives you a high.

Sativa primarily affects the mind and the emotions—energizing and uplifting your spirits.
Indica primarily affects the body—inducing relaxation, reducing pain and inflammation, and relaxing muscles.

So, for pain relief, a product made mostly from *Indica* would seem to be the answer for sports- and exercise-related injuries, but doctors suggest that for pain, you should use NSAIDs (nonsteroidal anti-inflammatory drugs) before trying *any* cannabis products. Common NSAIDs are *Aleve*, and *Ibuprofen*-type drugs such as *Advil* and *Motrin*. Besides, you should check that whatever variety of weed you choose won't have a bad reaction with any other medications you are taking.

Chewable **gummies** are the current popular (and discreet) way to consume weed; 5mg of THC per gummy is considered a low dose—and a low dose is the best way to test your tolerance as a beginner. You might even start with a 2.5mg dose. Gummies look like innocent candy, so ask what the dose per gummy is if someone offers you one. (When you buy them, the dose is noted on the packaging.) Unlike smoking or vaping, where the effect is experienced almost immediately, feeling the effect of a gummy (or other edibles) is delayed anywhere up to two hours, tempting you to eat another when nothing seems to be happening. Also, be aware that the gummy effect is much more long-lasting than smoking or vaping, so gummies may be the best way to relax sore muscles.

Some people use weed *before* working out, to calm any anxiety about going to the gym, making the exercise experience more pleasurable.

A couple of tennis "Ows." I asked my friend Ben Keyser (→) to tell me about tennis injuries. Here's what he said:

"Tennis causes injuries to ankles, knees and hips, through constant pounding against the court surface. Hard courts (cement) cause more knee and joint injuries than clay and grass, and that's why older (and now retired) stars like Federer and Nadal opted out of hard court events. The most common knee injury (↓) is a torn ACL. My worst injury was a knee problem that required surgery. It was the result of tight muscles in my quads and hips cutting off blood flow to my kneecap, causing part of the bone to "die" and become dislodged from the knee. As gruesome as it sounds, it's a much easier injury to recover from than an ACL tear."

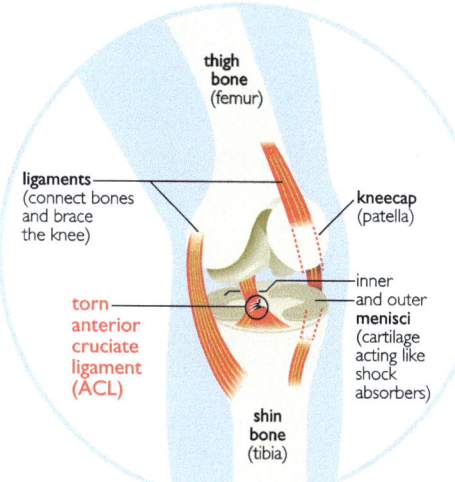

ligaments (connect bones and brace the knee)

thigh bone (femur)

kneecap (patella)

torn anterior cruciate ligament (ACL)

inner and outer menisci (cartilage acting like shock absorbers)

shin bone (tibia)

Ben (24) knows what he's tallking about when it comes to tennis. Starting at age 5, he rose quickly through the ranks of junior tennis, and was eventually ranked among the top 100 junior players in the US (and the number 1 high-school recruit in his home state of Virginia). Later, during his Junior year at college in California, he won the Championship-Flight singles title at the UCSB Classic.

Currently (2025), in between classes at graduate college, Ben is teaching and coaching tennis with adults and kids.

What about tennis elbow?

*"While playing tennis, I developed what should really be called golfer's elbow. The pain that people call tennis elbow is associated with tennis because it affects the **outside** of the elbow. Golfer's elbow affects the **inside** of the elbow (→). It's the result of hyper-extension of the arm among high-level players (me!) when hitting an overhand serve. You can look up images of pro players in the middle of*

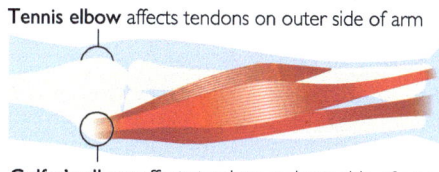

Tennis elbow affects tendons on outer side of arm

Golfer's elbow affects tendons on inner side of arm

hitting a serve and see the crazy angles that their elbows bend—almost (↓) backward. Golfers bend their elbows in a similar hyper-extension during a swing (←). It's relatively rare to see high-level tennis players experiencing tennis elbow; I suspect the injury among recreational players comes from poor backhand technique."

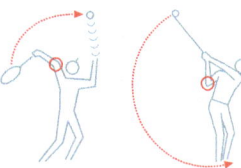

Friends

Fellow designers' fitness routines

I asked my infographic designer friends to show me what they did for exercise, if they did anything at all. It turns out that I know a kayaker, a dedicated runner, a competitive swimmer, a drummer, and a long-distance cyclist. Also a couch potato.

First, **Luigi Farrauto.** Luigi is a graphic designer and travel writer based in Milan, where he founded 100km Studio, a company specializing in narrating the world through maps, wayfinding, and travel guides.

"I don't like gyms, but if I need to move a bit I go out and walk, for hours. (Then I map it!)

When I was at MIT, I did an infographic presentation for my colleagues about some little exercises for the hands and neck while working at a computer. I suffered from carpal tunnel syndrome at the time so I needed them! (→)"

MICRO BREAKS
MAKE SMALL
EXERCISES.

Paul Mijksenaar (↓) studied industrial design at the Rietveld Academy in Amsterdam. After designing a series of prize-winning household appliances, he got involved with information design—in particular wayfinding—after being introduced to Jock Kinneir's new English road signs (1963). In 1986 he started his own office in Amsterdam which employs about 35 wayfinding designers with a branch in New York. He taught at Delft University and has several publications to his name.

"In Inspector Morse, *(the TV series), Morse uses what has become my favorite quote, and I've made it my motto ever since:*
'I detest gym, yoga, running, etc., etc. Exceptions are endless walking through cities and cycling, though they both became too tiring or too dangerous for people as old as I am.'" (Paul was born in 1944.)

RJ Andrews (→) San Francisco data storyteller RJ Andrews helps organizations solve high-stakes problems with visual metaphors and information graphics: charts, diagrams, and maps. He recently produced designs for The White House, Google, and MIT. He is the editor of *Information Graphic Visionaries*, a book series celebrating spectacular data visualization creators. His newest book is *Info We Trust: How to Create Value with Data Graphics* (Visionary Press, 2025).

As a tribute to Herbert Bayer's *Geo-Graphic Atlas,* RJ used Futura for his kayaking page.

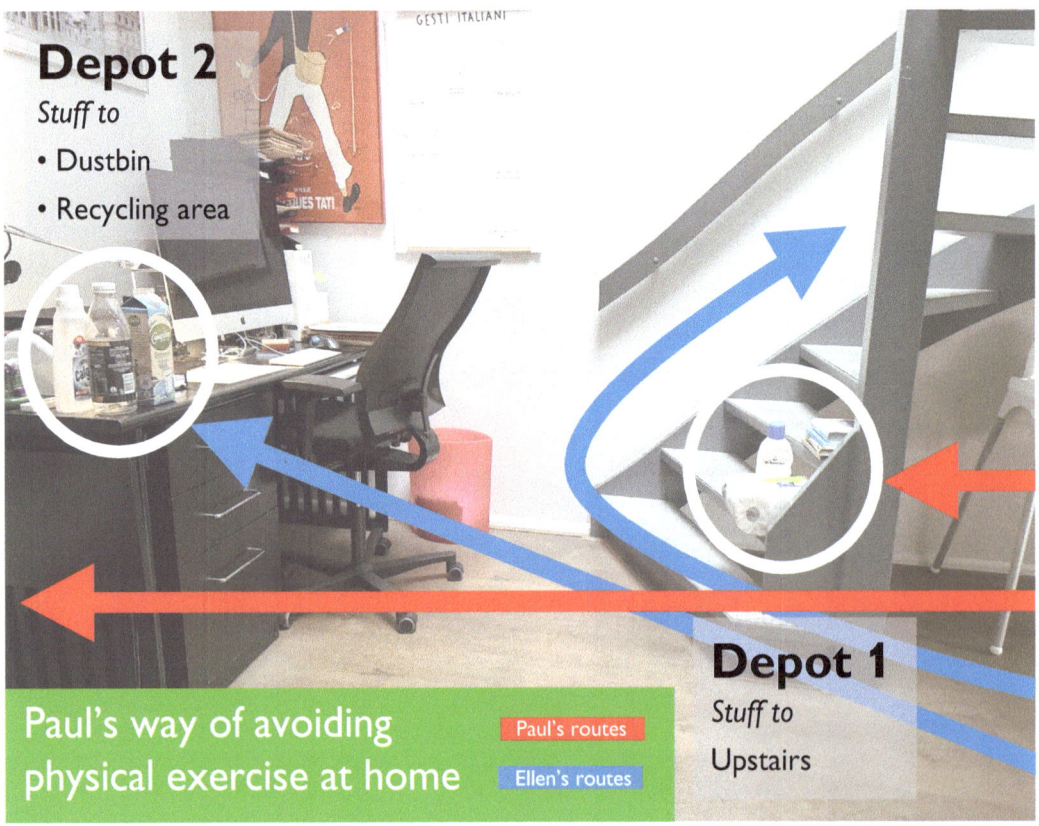

Depot 2
Stuff to
• Dustbin
• Recycling area

Depot 1
Stuff to
Upstairs

Paul's way of avoiding physical exercise at home

Paul's routes

Ellen's routes

bow

rudder

SOMA

BAY BRIDGE

MISSION
BAY

Crane
Cove

DOGPATCH

TIDES not only go in and
out, but also vary greatly
in their magnitude.

4 8 12 4

I roll the kayak to the
beach on a two-wheel
carriage, which
collapses and goes
inside my stern hatch
while I paddle.

In the first year of the Covid-19 pandemic, San Francisco opened a new beach two blocks from our flat—Crane Cove. Since then, I have kayaked a few times a week, year round. It keeps me sane.

Paddling also keeps me fit (and in great posture). Strangers smile when they see me and my gear rolling to or from the beach. They often strike up a conversation. Boat traffic and weather conditions are on my radar in a meaningful way.

My 14.5-foot touring kayak has a rudder that I control with my feet. I paddle it with a full-size carbon-fiber blade with a bent shaft, which helps keep my hands in alignment with my arms.

I keep paddling simple. No shoes. I don't touch my phone once I'm on the water except for the occasional snapshot. (I stopped logging journeys a long time ago.) A big hat and sunscreen protect me from the most dangerous threat out there.

I prefer a morning paddle on an incoming flood tide. This combines smooth water with a helping push after I turn back for the beach on my favorite route. But afternoons are fun, too: it is usually warmer and the winds blowing down Potrero Hill create fun chop to surf. Sometimes the whole water shimmers. Each paddle is unique.

Kayaking the Bay is an exceptional wildlife safari. I know all the sea lion nap spots. Harbor seals are curious, often popping up vertically near my kayak to take a look with their big dark eyes. I'm pretty good at telling pinnipeds apart, even at a big distance.

Pods of porpoise and dolphin are rare but exciting sights. Once, I chased a gray whale for a mile— an exhilarating experience that was tempered knowing that it was not supposed to be in the Bay.

Birds are just as interesting as marine mammals. The way a squadron of pelicans fly along the surface of the water is sublime. Sometimes they buzz me unexpectedly from my six o'clock. I delight when the dive-bombing terns return every year to fish. I imagine that a squawking blue heron flying overhead is a pterosaur.

And kayaking is where I do my best creative thinking. Whatever part of your mind gets to wander when you take a hot shower is also free to roam about when you kayak.—RJ Andrews

Ole Munk (→) is the Head of Design at *Kristeligt Dagblad,* an independent Danish national Newspaper.

"I've always been an extremely competitive person and as such I have been in love with sports— almost any kind of sports—ever since I was a young boy. Staying fit has never felt like a challenge. It started with football, then badminton; I even tried basketball but realized I was too short.

When I met Ulla, my second wife, my tennis career started. Now it's tennis in summer and (mostly) badminton in winter, even though with climate change we can actually play outdoor tennis more or less all year round.

We live close to the sea and I'm a keen swimmer. I ride a bike for all shorter trips—including part of the daily commute to my job in central Copenhagen (15 minutes each way).

For 25 years, I went on skiing holidays almost every year. But I tore my ACL 15 years ago, and my physiotherapist composed a daily training program to which I still adhere—just five minutes every morning, but it keeps the muscles around my knee in shape and allows me to keep playing tennis and badminton.

The wonderful thing about tennis, especially if you've started at a later stage in your life, is that you can keep learning and improving even though you get older, weaker, and slower. I read somewhere that tennis adds ten years to your life, and as it's also great fun, it's hard to see why anyone should not play tennis.

Forgot to mention: I always take the stairs, never the lift (but then again, we've got no skyscrapers)."

Heather Jones (↑) has 20+ years experience in media and publishing, and has been an Art Director, Dataviz Designer, Motion Graphics Producer and almost everything in between. Using whatever tools at hand—numbers, text, illustration, photographs, motion and sound (or all of the above)—she enjoys exploring the world, through graphics. At multiple news outlets, she has worked on a range of deep-dive journalistic projects in politics, science, health and culture, as well as corporate videos and international exhibitions. Based in Brooklyn, NY, she uses her own bright, dynamic designs as well as collaborations with other artists to tell data-driven stories. Her latest work, both personally driven and commissioned, includes collage and deadpan humor to engage the viewer in visually compelling ways. See more on Instagram and at msjonesnyc.com.

"I don't have an excuse to not work out when my gym is only a block away, and I've found exercise really clears my head, helps to solve design problems and even spurs new ideas when you step away, even for an hour. But sometimes we can't pull ourselves away from screens. I had a standing desk made because it makes it easier to move more when I work; I can sit down, stand, or move around as I've drawn in some low impact exercises here."

John Grimwade (↓) is an information designer (and friend), who has been making graphics for over 50 years.

"No one could describe me as a fitness enthusiast. I go to the gym only because it's good for me. Most days I'm there for an hour, inventing problems that have little to do with the gym itself. I'm a born worrier, so my thoughts even wander out into the parking lot."

GYM ANXIETY

Perhaps I'm just generally annoyed by having to work out, so I'm looking for problems. Here are a few of my many super-important issues at the health club.

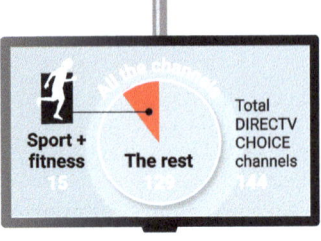

Sport + fitness | The rest

Total DIRECTV CHOICE channels

WORKOUT OVERLOAD

The TVs only show sport or fitness channels, but are hiding a lot of others.

ELLIPTICALLY-CHALLENGED

I was once shown the secrets of almost everything in the gym, however that was soon forgotten. Out of 48 cardio machines, I use just two ellipticals, and I don't really understand either of them.

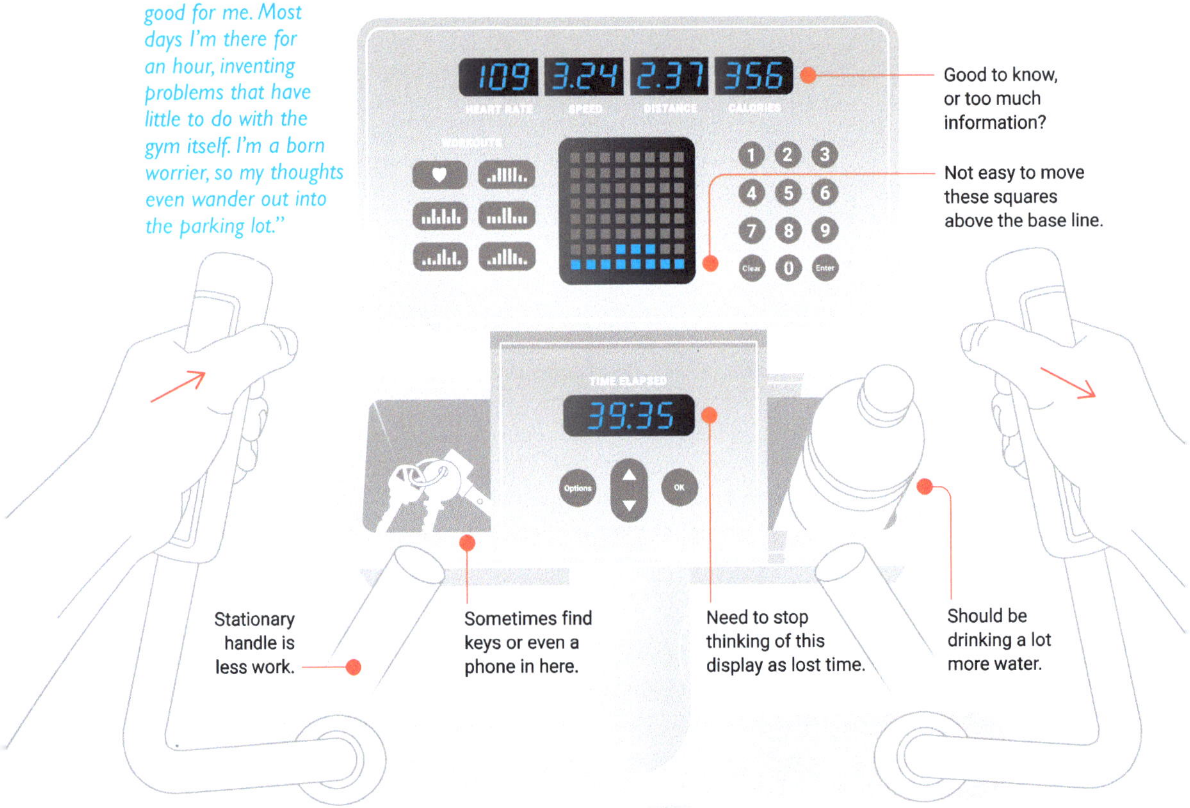

109 | 3.24 | 2.37 | 356
HEART RATE | SPEED | DISTANCE | CALORIES

WORKOUTS

Good to know, or too much information?

Not easy to move these squares above the base line.

TIME ELAPSED
39:35

Options | OK

Stationary handle is less work.

Sometimes find keys or even a phone in here.

Need to stop thinking of this display as lost time.

Should be drinking a lot more water.

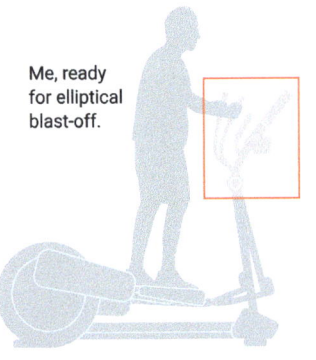

Me, ready for elliptical blast-off.

MUSICAL WAR

It's usually a volume battle between my earbuds and the house playlist.

Decibels

140

85 | 85

70

50

25

Whisper | Business office | City traffic | **EARBUDS** | **GYM SPEAKERS** | Jet engine

WATER PARK

The gym's parking lot is often partially-flooded. Easy to see why that's happening.

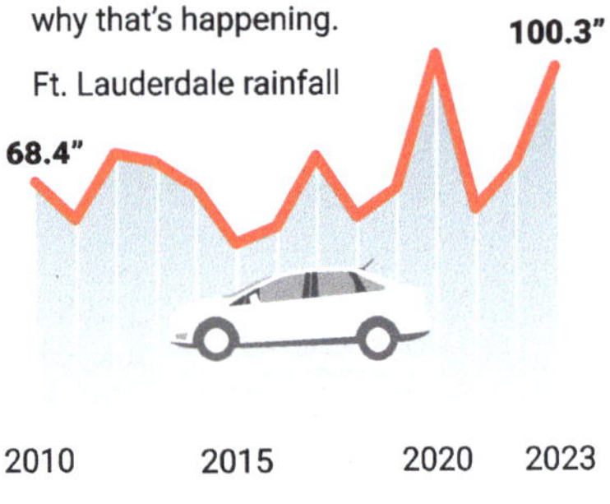

Ft. Lauderdale rainfall

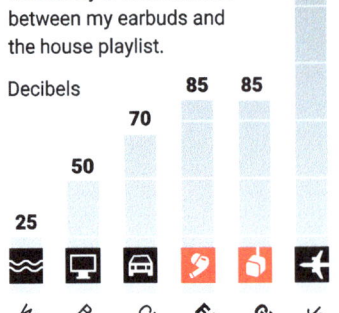

100.3"

68.4"

2010 | 2015 | 2020 | 2023

Dr. Kenneth Field (↑) cites maps as his passion, and profession. After 20 years teaching cartography and GIS in the UK, in 2011 Ken moved to California where he makes maps, talks, and writes about cartography. He is involved in the wider cartographic community with ICA, NACIS and BCS in particular, and previously as Editor of *The Cartographic Journal*.

He's won awards for maps, pedagogy, kitchen tiles, and his books *Cartography* and *Thematic Mapping*, and he leads a MOOC on Cartography which has been taken by over 200,000 students globally. He snowboards (reasonably), plays drums (badly), and supports his home-town football team Nottingham Forest.

"Drumming is a way of injecting breaks into the day (when I'm working at home). It's a good release from mental or practical blockages to whatever I'm working on.

My drums are a Roland V-Drums set. I had to swap my acoustic Yamaha set for electronic when we lived in a three-bed semi-detached property in London. Needless to say our neighbours didn't particularly enjoy the not-so-distant sound of drums.

Now that we live in a place in California with a bit of space, I added an amp and speakers so I didn't have to wear headphones."

Álvaro Valiño (→) is a graphics reporter for *The Washington Post* working from from his hometown, A Coruña, Galicia, Spain Formerly, he was head of the infographics department of the Spanish newspaper *Público*. He has freelanced for clients all around the world, including *National Geographic Magazine, The Guardian,* and *Corriere della Sera*.

The Washington Post used Álvaro's icons for their Paris Olympics coverage (↓),

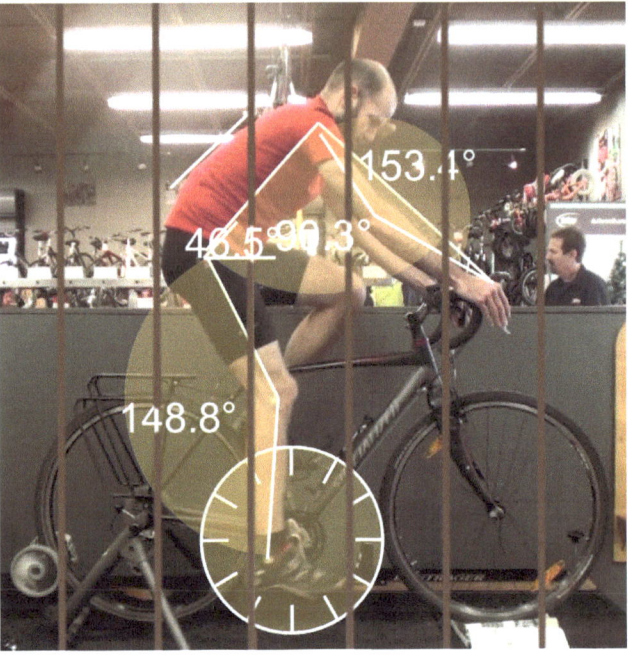

and added a similarly-styled graphic (↓) of *Pete*, who accompanied the adventures of graphics reporter Artur Galocha in Paris. Their reports added a sense of place and lots of fun to the regular sports coverage. The daily series was edited in the US office by Samuel Granados, with text by Bonnie Berkowitz.

Álvaro says:

"It was exhausting to do it every day! But I think it's a pity that innovation is usually regarded as being just about technology, when there are so many ways to do new things with narrative and visuals, and uncomplicated design."

"About staying fit myself: these days I have several joint issues, so I mostly stretch and use my body weight to keep in shape. I walk every day to the studio which is around 9,000 steps at a good pace (↓)

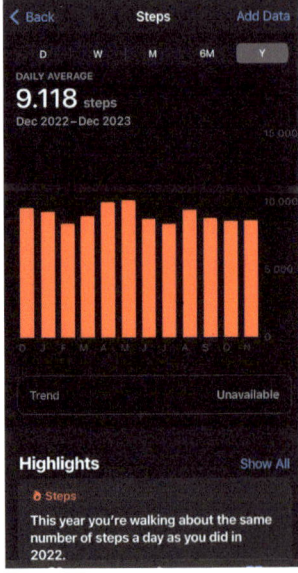

A while ago, before my knees started to tell me to take it easy, I used to ride my bike, and it developed into a passion; I did a solo tour in Morocco, and others in the Basque country and Sardinia, with great company.

This image (↑ with its strange grid) was generated by the software used by bike fitters when they adjusted my bike to my dimensions and flexibility. It shows the correct angles to keep me comfortable for long hours in the saddle.

I also did bike commuting in Madrid (not a bike-friendly city) during my time as the head of graphics at Público. One summer, my brilliant colleague Samuel Granados had the idea of doing a one-page infographic explaining how we commute to work, and encouraging readers to do the same. We jointly signed it as Alvaro Granados" (→).

Al trabajo en bici
POR ÁLVARO GRANADOS

El entorno donde vivo:

La bici en casa

Subir a la bici para ir al trabajo permite **comenzar el día a otro ritmo, sin los atascos en coche** o las aglomeraciones del metro. El viaje de ida es pausado, intentando evitar las grandes avenidas y el tráfico de calles principales. Lástima que no haya carril bici.

En el barrio

La bici permite una relación directa con el entorno y un **conocimiento más profundo de los diferentes modelos urbanos presentes en la ciudad.**

Del intrincado casco antiguo, a los espacios abiertos o las grandes avenidas y edificios de oficinas.

Con los demás

La velocidad a la que se mueve la bici **permite tomar el pulso a la vida en la calle.** Hace que sea mucho más cómodo visitar a amigos que vivan cerca sin necesidad de coger el coche, y evitándonos la espera buscando aparcamiento.

¿A casa? ←   → ¿A tomar algo?

VUELTA: 10,2 km | 34 min

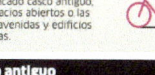
Casco antiguo

← Espacios cerrados. Vías de un carril

→ Camiones de reparto. Peatones temerarios ←

Nudos urbanos

← Espacios abiertos. Coches a más velocidad

→ A veces es necesario usar aceras.

Entorno laboral

← Edificios altos. Tráfico fluido

IDA: 9 km | 35 min

El entorno donde trabajo

Oficina y ejercicio físico

Trabajo en la oficina 8 horas sentado. Es necesario dedicar tiempo **para realizar ejercicio físico.** Algunos compañeros van al gimnasio en la hora de la comida, a otros les basta con el paseo en bici.

Ahorro de tiempo y energía

Se tarda menos en llegar al trabajo que los compañeros que viven en el mismo barrio y usan el coche o el transporte público. Se contamina **menos y se ahorra más energía.**

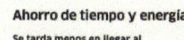

Vuelta a casa y relax

Después del ajetreo de la jornada laboral, vuelta a casa. **La bici me ayuda a desconectar.** A esa hora hay menos tráfico y se puede recorrer las grandes avenidas que se evitan a la mañana.

Andy Kirk is an independent data visualization, designer, consultant, trainer, lecturer, speaker, host of *Explore Explain,* and an all-round nice guy. His book, *Visualising Data: A Handbook for Data Driven Design* is the go-to book for students and professional designers. He has also published *The Seinfeld Chronicles,* for which the term *in-depth* is the understatement of all time.

Andy and I met at the Malofiej Conference in Spain, years ago, at that time not knowing we are both Yorkshiremen.

For this book, he created a detailed data visualization of his efforts to lose weight (→). I love his tiny icons— look closely: breakfast, lunch, and dinner—expertly rendered at 6pt type size.

But I had to ask Andy what was going on in the alcohol column on January 20th.

He says:
"Me and some mates went to watch a non-league football match in York, but it was postponed due to a frozen pitch, so we decided to pivot instead to spending the day and night in several of the City's historic pubs."

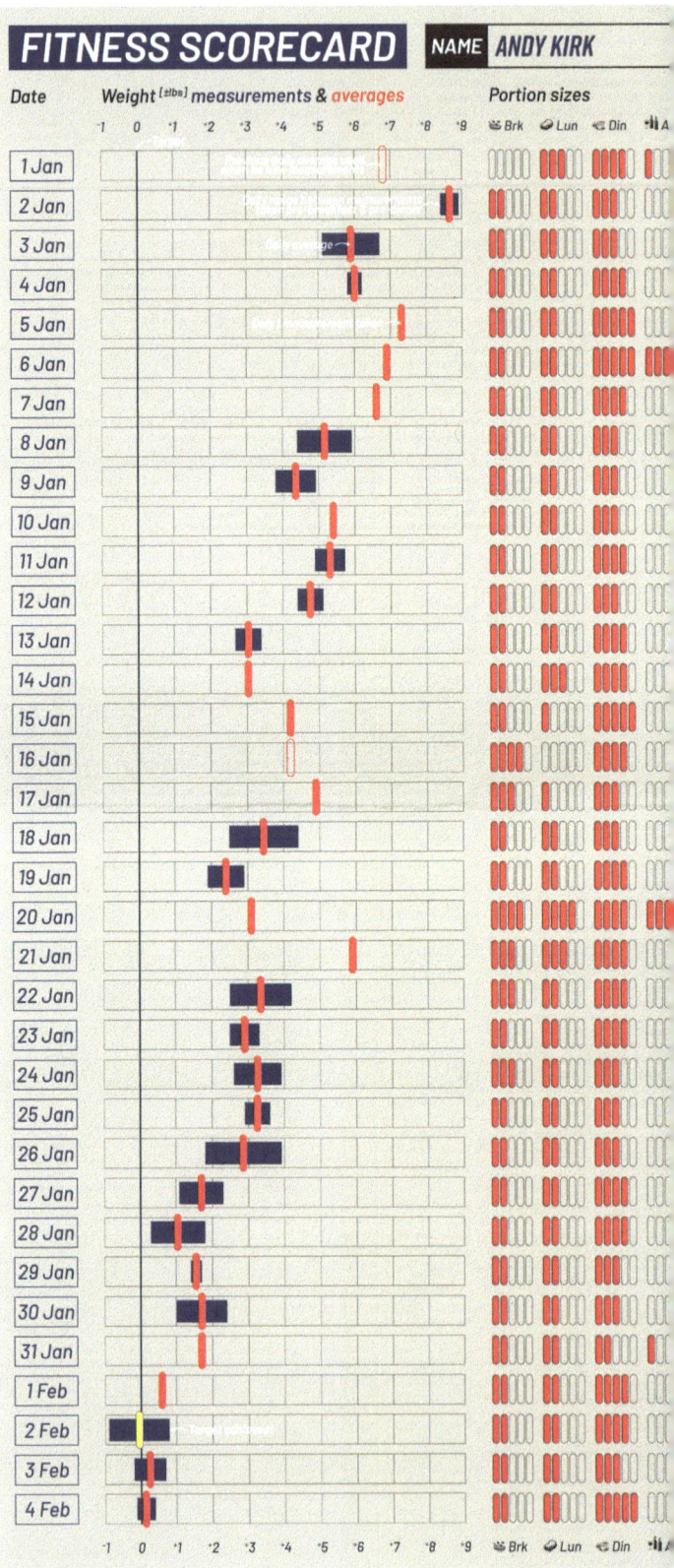

L FOLLOWING THE EXCESSES OF CHRISTMAS, IN THE FACE OF UNFAVOURABLE WINTER CONDITIONS AND A BUSY WORK SCHEDULE, AIM TO REACH MY TARGET WEIGHT WITHIN ONE MONTH THROUGH A COMBINATION OF HEALTHIER DIET, SMALLER PORTIONS, AND INCREASED FREQUENCY OF WALKS AND RUNNING ACTIVITIES.

Runs	Run characteristics		Conditions

Time / Pace	Run	Speed (downhill/uphill/flat)	Distance	Weather / Temp
21m43s 5:47/km	Run D ↑27m ↓32m		3.75km	🌙☁ 6°
23m05s 5:51/km	Run H ↑32m ↓38m		3.95km	🌙⛅ 5°
22m33s 5:43/km	Run H ↑32m ↓38m		3.95km	🌙⛅ 1°
25m08s 5:17/km	Run G ↑42m ↓66m		4.75km	🌙⛅ 2°
25m33s 5:23/km	Run G ↑42m ↓66m		4.75km	🌙☁ 6°
22m16s 5:38/km	Run H ↑32m ↓38m		3.95km	🌙☁ 1°
23m08s 5:51/km	Run H ↑32m ↓38m		3.95km	☀❄ 0°
22m39s 5:44/km	Run H ↑32m ↓38m		3.95km	🌙❄ 3°
22m03s 5:35/km	Run H ↑32m ↓38m		3.95km	☀🌧 9°
22m21s 5:39/km	Run H ↑32m ↓38m		3.95km	🌙☁ 9°
22m13s 5:37/km	Run H ↑32m ↓38m		3.95km	🌙⛅ 5°
24m53s 5:14/km	Run G ↑42m ↓66m		4.75km	🌙⛅ 6°
22m34s 5:43/km	Run H ↑32m ↓38m		3.95km	🌙⛅ 11°
21m56s 5:33/km	Run H ↑32m ↓38m		3.95km	🌙⛅ 5°
14m37s 5:37/km	Run F ↑19m ↓25m		2.60km	🌙☁ 7°
22m02s 5:35/km	Run H ↑32m ↓38m		3.95km	🌙☁ 12°
25m12s 5:29/km	Run A ↑47m ↓50m		4.60km	🌙☁ 9°
14m45s 5:40/km	Run F ↑19m ↓25m		2.60km	☀🌧 11°

Bonnie Berkowitz and **Laura Stanton** of *The Washington Post*'s infographics department put this great poster together, featuring their office colleagues. They tested the exercises in and around their cubicles to see which ones people could incorporate into a work-day. (They note that their observations aren't scientific, but are definitely real.)

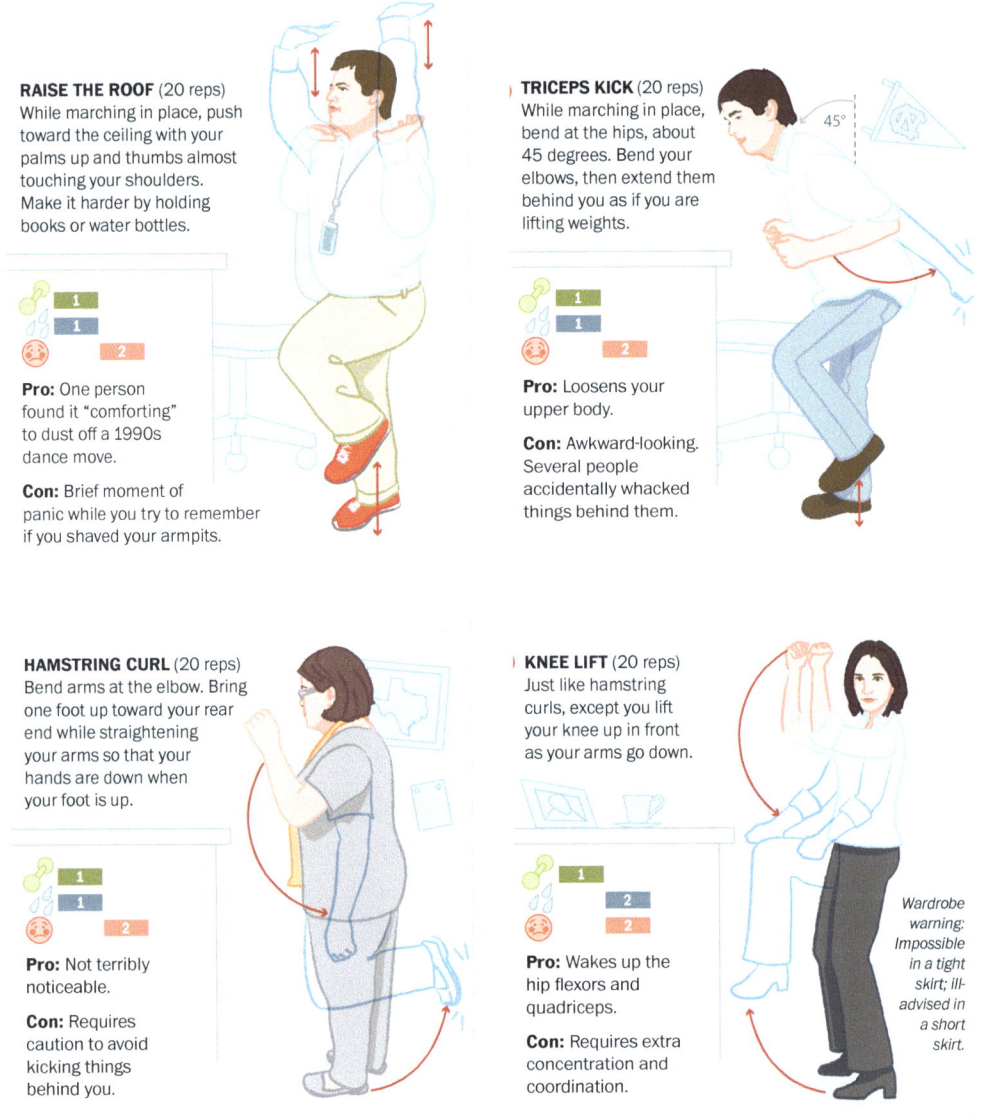

RAISE THE ROOF (20 reps)
While marching in place, push toward the ceiling with your palms up and thumbs almost touching your shoulders. Make it harder by holding books or water bottles.

Pro: One person found it "comforting" to dust off a 1990s dance move.

Con: Brief moment of panic while you try to remember if you shaved your armpits.

TRICEPS KICK (20 reps)
While marching in place, bend at the hips, about 45 degrees. Bend your elbows, then extend them behind you as if you are lifting weights.

45°

Pro: Loosens your upper body.

Con: Awkward-looking. Several people accidentally whacked things behind them.

HAMSTRING CURL (20 reps)
Bend arms at the elbow. Bring one foot up toward your rear end while straightening your arms so that your hands are down when your foot is up.

Pro: Not terribly noticeable.

Con: Requires caution to avoid kicking things behind you.

KNEE LIFT (20 reps)
Just like hamstring curls, except you lift your knee up in front as your arms go down.

Pro: Wakes up the hip flexors and quadriceps.

Con: Requires extra concentration and coordination.

Wardrobe warning: Impossible in a tight skirt; ill-advised in a short skirt.

Sources: Tony Yancey, professor of health studies at UCLA and author of the get-moving book "Instant Recess"; Alice Burron, exercise physiologist and spokeswoman for the American Council on Exercise; Catrine Tudor-Locke, who studies walking behavior at Pennington Biomedical Research

	NOT TOO		VERY
Difficult?	1	2	3
Sweaty?	1	2	3
Humiliating?	1	2	3

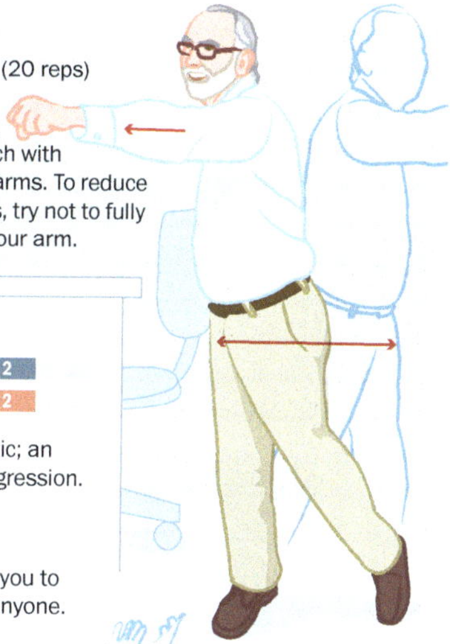

PUNCHING (20 reps)
While rocking foot to foot, punch with alternating arms. To reduce elbow stress, try not to fully straighten your arm.

1	
	2
	2

Pro: Cathartic; an outlet for aggression.

Con: Most workplaces do not allow you to actually hit anyone.

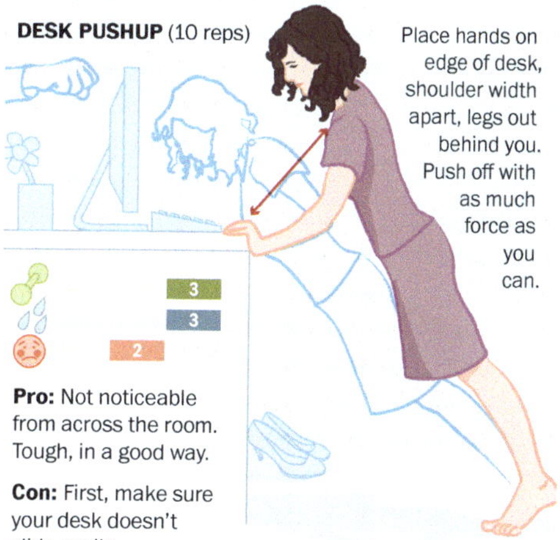

DESK PUSHUP (10 reps)
Place hands on edge of desk, shoulder width apart, legs out behind you. Push off with as much force as you can.

	3
	3
	2

Pro: Not noticeable from across the room. Tough, in a good way.

Con: First, make sure your desk doesn't slide easily.

JUMP SQUATS (10)
Make sure you have space in front of you. Bend into a half-squat with your arms behind you, then jump and swing your arms up as if you're celebrating.

Wardrobe warning: Major risk of exposure in a billowy skirt or untucked shirt.

	3
	3
	3

Pro: Best calorie-burner of the moves we tried.

Con: Tall people (or high-hopping short people) will hit eight-foot ceilings.

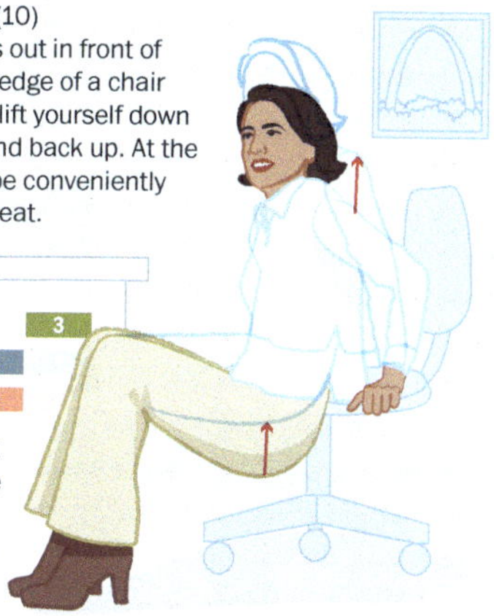

CHAIR DIPS (10)
With your legs out in front of you, grab the edge of a chair (or desk) and lift yourself down in front of it and back up. At the end, you will be conveniently back in your seat.

	3
	2
	2

Pro: The most discreet of the bunch. Really works triceps.

Con: Can bother wrists. Be careful if your chair has wheels!

In my region of New York's Hudson Valley the growing season extends from April through September. Seed catalogs arrive soon after and the most exercise I get is removing the cat from the growing pile.

Digging beds and hauling compost before the growing season begins comes next. The muscles you've used will make themselves known by morning!

Planting cold weather crops like lettuce and peas, irrigating and keeping the beds weed-free will test your back.

HUFFING & PUFFING IN THE GARDEN

= 1 year

= 1 month

Cutting back and hauling away overgrown spring foliage to make way for warm weather crops and many trips to the brush pile or compost heap help tone those arms.

Planting warm weather crops like tomatoes and beans means more irrigating and tying up growing plants with supports.

Harvest time at last!

Putting the garden to bed for the season, planting bulbs and garlic to overwinter, raking leaves off the lawn to where they can serve as mulch and overwintering spots for insects. Whew! Time for a rest...

Renée Klein's (↑) lifelong love of gardening began as a child with her grandmother as mentor. Between planting and digging she has worked as an art director, designer, and infographics designer at *The Boston Globe, The Real Paper, Time* and *Fortune* magazines. Her illustrations have appeared in *Rolling Stone, The New York Times, Time,* and *Vanity Fair;* on book jackets for Knopf, and posters for Levi's jeans. Married to illustrator Terry Allen she now lives and gardens in New York's Hudson Valley.

Sergio Peçanha (↓ →) is a graphics editor and visual columnist for *The Washington Post*. He uses illustrations, maps, charts, and animations to tell stories. Before the *Post*, he was a graphics editor at *The New York Times*. Peçanha has the same ç as "façade," and it rhymes with "lasagna".

"I do several things to stay sane and keep healthy. I practice some yoga; here I am doing a standing forward bend (↑).

Also, I'm a swimmer, three times a week. I'm not the fastest, but I am enthusiastic about it!

In July, 2024, I participated in a 6k open water race in Paraty, a city about four hours south of Rio. This is me at the finish line (←).

An interesting thing: as I trained for the event, I had to do many long, intense swim sessions. One day, about a month before the race, I was going about my day after my morning swim and realized that I was feeling a bit weird. I was euphoric and it lasted hours... It was strange. So I asked around, Googled and discovered my diagnosis: I had been "afflicted" by runner's high, a feeling of euphoria that sometimes people feel after intense exercise.

So I had found a natural way to literally feel high in life!"

Freestyle (6.55km)

7:41AM–9:54 AM

↑ Paraty-Mirim Beach

Workout Time	Distance
2:13:09	6.60KM

Active Calories	Total Calories
1,752CAL	2,014CAL

Avg. Pace	Avg. Heart Rate
2'02"/100m	156BPM

(←) This is the time on my watch (not official) with the actual distance that I swam (6.6km).

Jason Forrest (↓) is a data visualization expert in New York City working at the intersection of business, culture, and data. He is the founder of the Jason Forrest Agency, focused on solving complex problems in business and industry.

"I've been a runner for many years now and my schedule fluctuates based on my meetings and ongoing projects. I have tried to run three times a week, on this 4K route for the last several years, but there's always a level of variability based on time, weather, and appointments.

One of the best things about living in Manhattan is the ability to run in Central Park—while it is literally a joy every time, it is flat as a pancake, and I've wondered what the elevations were like for my run, so mapping it proves it's a smidge more varied than I assumed."

Running Route

Elevation
55 m
53 m
43 m
33 m

Legend		
27	RUNNING	
32	WALKING	
8	OTHER PHYSICAL ACTIVITY	
23	IMPORTANT WORK DAY (Big meeting, conference, workshop)	
15	WORK TRAVEL	
12	HOLIDAY/VACATION	

Sunday	Monday	Tuesday	Wednesday	Thursday	Friday	Saturday	
				1	2	3	AUGUST
4	5	6	7	8	9	10	
11	12	13	14	15	16	17	
18	19	20	21	22	23	24	
25	26	27	28	29	30	31	
1	2	3	4	5	6	7	SEPTEMBER
8	9	10	11	12	13	14	
15	16	17	18	19	20	21	
22	23	24	25	26	27	28	
29	30	1	2	3	4	5	OCTOBER
6	7	8	9	10	11	12	
13	14	15	16	17	18	19	
20	21	22	23	24	25	26	
27	28	29	30	31	1	2	NOVEMBER
3	4	5	6	7	8	9	
10	11	12	13	14	15	16	
17	18	19	20	21	22	23	
24	25	26	27	28	29	30	

Sunday	Monday	Tuesday	Wednesday	Thursday	Friday	Saturday
8 runs	4 runs	5 runs	2 runs	5 runs	3 runs	0 runs
5 walks	7 walks	5 walks	4 walks	5 walks	2 walks	5 walks
1 other	1 other	1 other	3 others	0 other	0 other	2 other

Next

Beyond science (and life?)

There will always be new machines, fads, regimes, and diets to make us feel guilty about not being fit. Here are some ideas that might be pseudo-science or just plain silly.

Stuff that Dr. K artfully calls nonscience (pronounced *non-shunce*).

Longevity

Living a long life seems to be a current popular quest—mostly by people with lots of money; private longevity clinics charge from $5,000 to $50,000 a year. For the less well off, a public facility for healthy longevity at the Mayo Clinic in Rochester, Minnesota charges far less. Here are some ways to bring you a few extra birthdays.

Orchiectomy

In 2012, a study published in the journal *Current Biology* claimed that the path to a longer life is castration. The study cited the ancient royal practice of gelding men in order to make them more trustworthy and better suited to court service—because they had lessened sexual desire. But it also led to longer lives for the eunuchs, and that's the part of the study that interested modern researchers. On average, they found castrated men lived 14 years longer than other men. Researcher Cat Bohannon, who recently cited the study, says: *"Men go through life with two little death nuggets"*—a reference to the apparently malign effects of testosterone.

Yikes! Although I can think of a few men for whom this procedure is karmically deserved. On the other hand, if it makes them live longer, forget it.

Freezing

So here's an even more drastic way to "live" longer: you die, but are immediately frozen, in the hope that you can be resuscitated in the future. The *Cryonics Institute* in Michigan charges $28,000 to freeze your body and store it indefinitely. They currently store 200 bodies; 2,000 living people have signed up. *Alcor Life Extension*

Foundation was incorporated in California in 1972, and charges considerably more—$200,000 to store your whole body, or $80,000 for just your brain—to be frozen to −196°C (−384.8°F).

Storing the brain to be brought back to life when science is ready got me wondering what that future "life" might be. How will the human race evolve in the far future? We are already a sedentary lot, relying on machines to do everything for us—self-isolating, apparently happy to be alone with electronic devices, playing games, emailing, ordering everything from food to footwear, watching TV. Might we evolve into couchbrains (←)? No need for anyone to go anywhere … we are almost there now: kept busy with individual, wearable virtual reality (VR) goggles (and they will surely soon be controlled by thoughts alone). No body, no arms or legs, no movement, no exercise … no *books* about exercise.

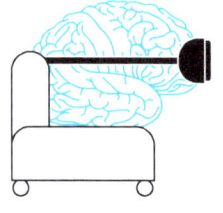

This scenario is depicted in Pixar's 2008 animated film *WALL-E*.

The case of Jeanne Calment

In 1997, Jeanne Calment died at 122, the oldest age ever recorded. Some researchers, notably Nikolay Zak, a gerontologist at the Moscow Society of Naturalists, believe it was Jeanne's daughter Yvonne who died in 1997. Yvonne had assumed her mother's identity to avoid tax inheritance when Jeanne actually died—if she did—in 1934.

Zak's 2019 paper was met with considerable resistance, including common sense; for instance, the identity switch meant that Yvonne lived with her father *as his wife* until he died in 1942, and no one noticed or raised red flags? Zak's view: everyone in the French town of Arles (pop. 50,000) did know, and kept quiet, or believed Yvonne had died in 1934, and that their grand old Dame was Jeanne herself. Zak has admitted to Reuters that he does not have "cast-iron proof."

Here's a timeline to help keep the dates straight:

		(age)		(age)
Jeanne Calment	1875	1934 (59)	1997 (122)	
Jeanne's daughter, Yvonne	1898	1934 (36)	1997 (99)	
Jeanne's husband, Fernand	1875	1942 (73)		

The controversial biogerontologist Dr. Aubrey de Grey, is also interested in the case that Zak makes. In 2008, de Grey claimed that the first person to live to 1,000 was probably alive already, and was at that time aged between 50 and 60. More recently he has claimed that by 2100, humans could live to 5,000.

Whatever you think about longevity, it has some big money behind it: PayPal co-founder Peter Thiel has given millions of dollars To SENS (Strategies for Engineered Negligible Senescence), the research foundation that de Grey founded in 2009. And Google (Alphabet Inc.) has invested $1.5 billion in its own Calico Life Sciences, which is dedicated to answering questions about the biology of aging.

The Longevity Escape Velocity Foundation

Founded in 2022 by Dr. de Grey, who is the President and Chief Science Officer, the Longevity Escape Velocity (LEV) foundation suggests a hypothetical way that we may someday reach a point where aging is "optional." The idea is a reference to *escape velocity* in physics—the minimum speed required for an object to indefinitely move out of the gravitational pull of a body. LEV states that medical advances in life expectancy—not from birth—in a given year, will extend life expectancy more than the year that just passed. Got that?

Futurist Ray Kurzweil (of *Singularity* fame) has predicted that LEV will be reached before we know it. In 2024, he wrote that it would occur between 2029 and 2035.

In 2024, the US Census claimed there were 100,000 Americans aged 100 or older, and that by 2054 that number will be 400,000.

Don't Die

While Zak, de Grey, Kurzweil and others deal in possibilities for the future, Bryan Johnson practices (some) of what he advocates. Born in 1977, he is the founder of *Blueprint,* and his followers wear black t-shirts with *DON'T DIE* in bold white letters on them. While Johnson's diet protocols do praise the idea of "healthspan"—that is, good quality of life in older age versus a traditional lifespan—it is actually the living longer part that he's really promoting. He reportedly spends $2 million a year on treatments to help himself live longer. They have included a plasma transplant from his teenage son. (He stopped when he realized it wasn't working.)

There's a Netflix documentary about Johnson, *Don't Die: The Man Who Wants to Live Forever.* His non-disclosure requirements are being challenged by employees.

Scientific data doesn't support Johnson's claims of how to reverse aging, but his comeback line is simple: "You'll die before you get a scientific consensus" on his diet, which is an odd statement given

Among Johnson's daily
intake of 2,250 calories is
Nutty pudding (433 cals).

In a blender, put:
50-100 ml macadamia
nut milk
3tbsp ground
macadamia nuts
2tsp ground walnuts
2tsp chia seeds
2tsp ground flaxseed
1/4 brazil nut
1tbsp dark cocoa
1tsp sunflower lecithin
1/2tsp Ceylon cinnamon
1/2 cup berries
3 cherries
2oz pomegranate juice
—Recipe from Colin Keeley.

his own t-shirt's catchphrase. You just have to trust him, and his *literally* nutty food advice (←), and shell out $300+ a month to get a supply of his supplements.

A different view of long life

Leonard Hayflick's work—resulting in what is now called the *Hayflick Limit*—bugged the live-forever theorists (and other assorted nut jobs). His 2024 *NY Times* obituary read: *Leonard Hayflick, Who Discovered Why No One Lives Forever, Dies at 96.*

This is what he discovered, in the early 1960s, while he was at the Wistar Institute, at the University of Pennsylvania:

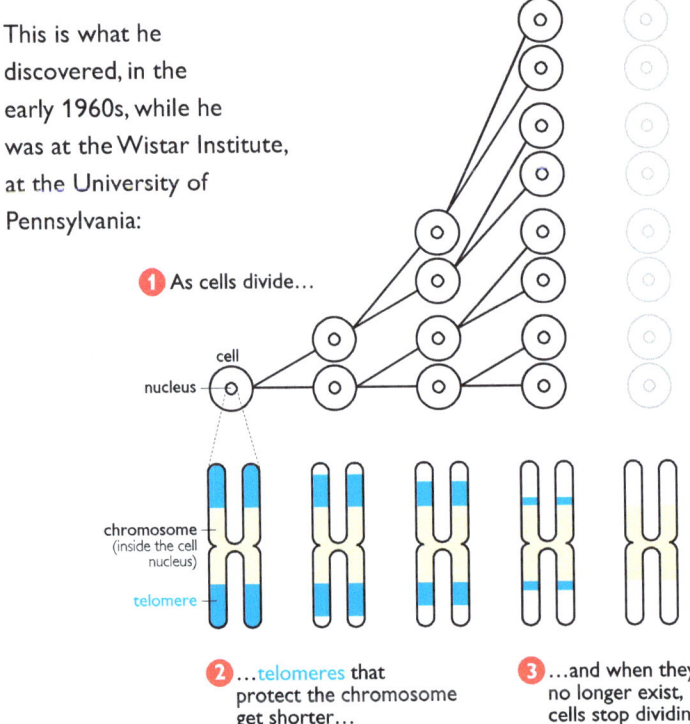

1 As cells divide…

cell

nucleus

chromosome
(inside the cell
nucleus)

telomere

2 …telomeres that protect the chromosome get shorter…

3 …and when they no longer exist, cells stop dividing.

Normal cells divide about 60 times before they age—they have reached the *Hayflick Limit*. That's why no engineering, or exercise, or diet can push life beyond about 125 years (much to the annoyance of people who believe we will one day be immortal).

Normal long life without dying, hypotheticals, and "supplements"

Richard Morgan was a World Champion indoor rower. He lived to 93, having started to row at 73. He exercised 40 minutes a day, rowing about 18.5mi (30km) every week; most of the time with a relatively easy stroke, then for a short period at a faster pace, and finally rowing flat out, as fast as he could go, for about five minutes. Morgan prolonged his life, and its quality—his "healthspan"—with rigorous exercise, and also with a high-protein diet. (I imagine he had some good genes to start with, too). I know this is only a sample of one, but it shows there's hope for all of us.

At eye-level on most gym rowing machines there's a small screen showing calories used, distance traveled, etc., together with a bar chart of how much energy you are putting into each pull. Using the bars in the chart, I try to "draw" pictures on it—here, a profile (→) of a person looking up, laughing—by pulling harder or less hard to make the bars taller or shorter. It's a bit silly, but it keeps me concentrating.

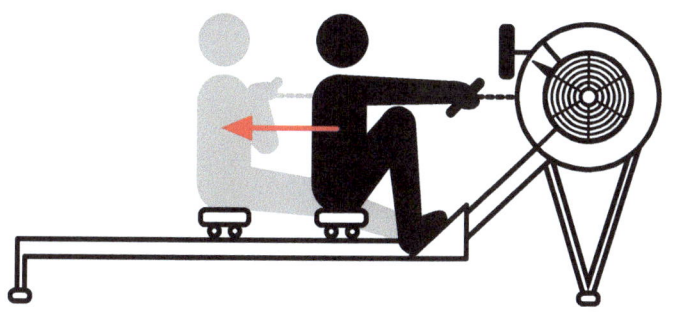

Exercise pills

Will we ever be able to take a pill and skip exercising?

Based on writings from several centuries BC, a man called Wei Boyang made a *Pill of Immortality* (in Chinese: *Xiandan*). It was thought to grant both physical and spiritual immortality. Until AD 500, Chinese alchemists kept searching for Boyang's secret formula. The first Emperor of China, Qin Shi Huang really wanted them to find it. He died at age 49 in 210 BC, and a theory about the cause was that he was poisoned by an "immortality" elixir containing mercury.

Today, scientists are searcing for "exercise mimetics," substances that can stand in for the health benefits of all those trips to the gym—or anything you are doing to keep fit. *Aerium Therapeutics* aim to commercialize *Irisin*, a hormone released by your muscles when you exercise. *Irisin* might be taken as injections, or, eventually, the magic exercise pill.

The proposed treatment appears to have similarities with *Ozempic* and other GLP-1 drugs, which were first designed to treat diabetes, but subsequently have been used as weight-loss medications. The initial use for *Irisin* was to combat amyloid plaques in the brain that cause *Alzheimer's disease*.

Virtual Reality fitness

Jane Fonda teams up with *Supernatural,* a division of Meta.

In what their advertisements say is "the end of boring cardio,"

Supernatural, a VR fitness service, offers "revolutionary" workouts in exotic locations via a wireless *Meta Quest* headset. Some workouts are led by Jane Fonda, whose videos in the 1980s were an earlier—and altogether more human—fitness revolution. If exercising in front of a picture of the Great Wall of China, while wearing a bulky headset is your thing, you might like this.

Artificial intelligence

Ai gym

Since I invariably use sans serif fonts in books and diagrams, I prefer to see the words artificial and intelligence shortened to Ai (capital A, lowercase i) instead of AI to avoid any typographic confusion like this:
AI (capital I)
Al (lowercase L)
A1 (A-one)

Lumin Fitness is not another at-home remote exercise program, like *Supernatural,* it's an actual brick-and-mortar place to go to work out, by yourself or in a group. It's all powered by the *Lumin Operating System,* downloaded onto your phone. At their studio in Las Colinas, Texas there is a bright, seasonally-themed wall-to-wall LED screen, and you are assigned a position in front of your own Ai trainer. If you are in a group class, everyone is doing the same set of exercises, but you have chosen your own music soundtrack, and training style (for instance, "Rex" is a hard-driving drill sergeant, while "Emma" is more of an encouraging best friend; there is also a real live trainer in the studio, in case you need technical help). Your performance is tracked and you get guidance and feedback as the class progresses.

Let's Get Infografit

The idea of working out with an Ai trainer might be appealing to some, but there's a different aspect of Ai—generative Ai—that troubles me. This book is not written by, or with the help of Ai. Instead it is written with Ni—and that's not Ni as in Nickel; nor is it the word used by the Knights Who Say "Ni" in the movie *Monty Python and the Holy Grail.* The Ni I have used is Nigel intelligence.

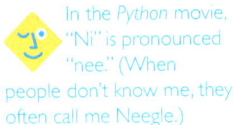 In the *Python* movie, "Ni" is pronounced "nee." (When people don't know me, they often call me Neegle.)

Big Tech would like us to think that Ai is *learning* from the source material it is being fed. But it isn't learning, it's *copying*—without understanding. It doesn't give credit most of the time, and if that's not bad enough, there's a tendency for it to "hallucinate" (←).

Hallucinations are what Ai systems sometimes produce—text not based on facts. What ChatGPT does is predict the next word in a sentence, the way your smart phone does. And just as you are annoyed when your phone suggests something you didn't want to say, Ai generative systems get things wrong—they make stuff up. The trouble is, you don't know it's wrong because it *sounds* good.

While reading about health and fitness, and then writing this book, I looked at, summarized, and borrowed from lots of already published articles and books about exercise and fitness (there's a list on page 154). Just what Ai would have done, you might say. Here's the difference between Ni and Ai. With Ni, I do what any writer does: I bring my own experience. Artificial intelligence doesn't have any experience, or intelligence, of its own. The name says it all—it's *artificial*—not real. Perhaps in the future Ai will move beyond what appears to be a form of plagiarism and we'll have to think of another name for it. There's got to be a more truthful one. Who wants something that proclaims itself to be *artificial?* (And *intelligence?* That's offensively misleading.)

is a baby. But it's here, and it may grow up. All parents think their toddler is a wonder. They have great hopes for his or her future. This baby is yelling at us—at the moment. I'm dreading what Ai will be like as a teenager, and I hope its parents will know how to deal with that. Perhaps, when Ai is old enough to leave the house, it will settle into the bureaucracy of adulthood, doing boring, repetitive paperwork that could save millions of hours of office work so that people can go and EXERCISE! I'm trying to be as optimistic as possible about the future (pessimism is not good for your health). Besides, I may be wrong. But I still have to ask, will Ai ever be a truly independent, thinker? Tony Fernandes, founder of *UserExperience.ai,* says: "…no matter how sophisticated the Ai process is, humans will need to stay involved, and provide insight."

The same way that I don't trust Ai to help me to write, I would approach Ai trainers with skepticism. Can you really leave your exercise choices to a machine?

In 2024, Geoffrey Hinton, shared the Nobel Prize in Physics with John Hopfield for their work on artificial neural networks. The prize was a surprise for Hinton, because in 2023 he had resigned from his position as a researcher at Google, warning that he feared Ai could wipe out humanity. Here is an excerpt from an interview with Cade Metz of *The New York Times* following the announcement:

Metz: "…*you have won a Nobel for helping to create a technology that you now worry will cause serious danger for humanity. How do you feel about that?*"
Hinton: "*Having the Nobel Prize could mean that people will take me more seriously.*"
Metz: "*Take you more seriously when you warn of future dangers?*"
Hinton: "*Yes.*"

Ask Google "What's the difference between Ai and generative Ai?" and you will get this Ai-generated (!) answer:
"Traditional Ai analyzes data to make predictions, while generative Ai creates new data based on existing data."

Always ahead of his time, George Orwell warned us about something like Ai in his 1946 essay, *Books and Cigarettes:* "*It would probably not be beyond human ingenuity to write books by machinery.*"
Next time I am anywhere in the vicinity of Sutton Courtenay, near Oxford, England, I'll help him turn over in his grave. (The tombstone has his real name, of course, Eric Arthur Blair.)

Artists and writers see Ai as a predatory threat, while scientists see possibilities for faster life-saving drug development (to cite just one example) that would take years of research without the help of Ai.

10
TEN
Et cetera

And the rest ... bonus content!

When I'm writing, I collect all sorts of stuff in the hope it'll find a place somewhere in the book. Some of it might be on the outskirts of a subject, but still interesting, and some is merely fun (→). My first mentor in this field, Brian Haynes, with whom I interned in 1965 at *The Sunday Times Magazine* in London, had this mantra driving his art direction: *put everything in; if it interests you, some of your readers will also find it interesting.*

You might say this whole chapter warrants the yellow imp. But if we can't have a little fun, life isn't worth living, right?

Some bicycles
These examples don't exactly fit the idea of "exercise" I have been going on about. But I like them, anyway. This one is from 1939.

The Reuleaux Bike looks uncomfortable (if not impossible) to ride, but the clever mechanical suspension (↓) makes it relatively smooth, even though the wheels—*reuleaux* triangles, which have a constant width, like a circle—do not rotate around a fixed center, instead, they move up and down, as the rider pedals forward.

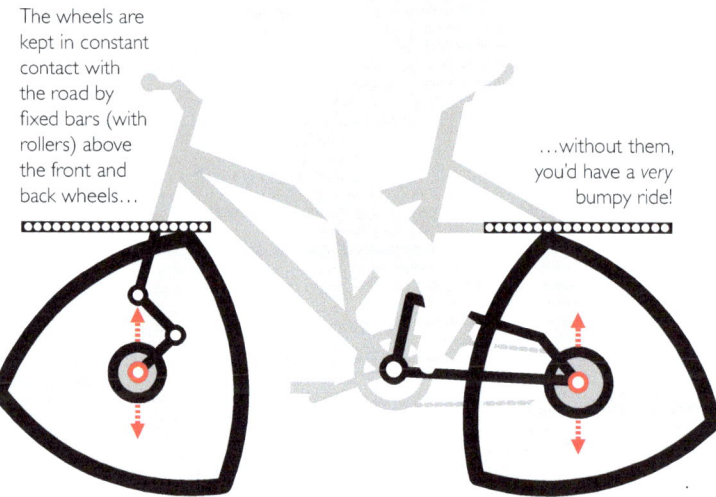

The wheels are kept in constant contact with the road by fixed bars (with rollers) above the front and back wheels…

…without them, you'd have a *very* bumpy ride!

How to construct a Reuleaux triangle.

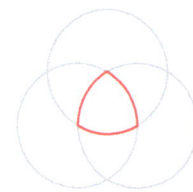

The wheels are named after a 19th century German engineer, Franz Reuleaux—who studied how different shapes affected motion—although from a much earlier time, there are Gothic church windows of this shape, and Leonardo da Vinci used the triangles for a map projection.

The Big Bike Orchestra is a Polish pop-folk band formed in 2021 in Bydgoszcz. The band performs in cities all over Europe.

My favorite bike image is Daniel Utz's simple, "pixellated" symbol (↑).
You are more likely to see it reduced to this conventional icon size (→),
…but doesn't it look great bigger?

See Daniel's work at danielutz.de

In contrast to Daniel's bike icon, the
Big Bike Orchestra's logo is a different,
more realistic approach to icon- and
symbol-making—a simple silhouette.

Stick figures

As an information graphics designer, I try to find interesting ways to see and draw the things that people ask me to explain. I often start out with the simplest way: stick figures.

When I first started with a fitness trainer, I made rough visual notes of the exercises he was teaching me (↓) so I would remember them on the days when I was alone in the gym.

Yes, I could have found the moves I was trying to remember in an app on my phone, but as with most note-taking, I remember the points more clearly when I actually write or draw them by hand.

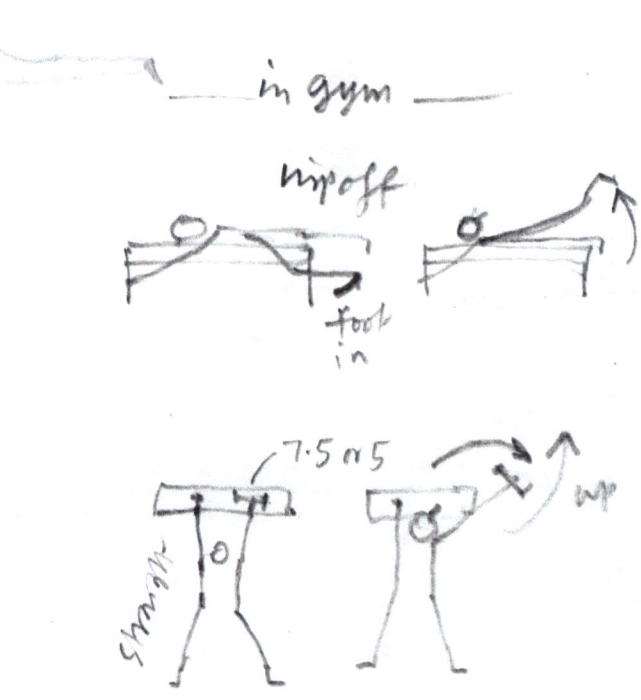

In Chapter 6, there's an exercise program (Three-Rep) populated with a finished version of stick figures. These (←) are some of my first attempts to make a cohesive group of "people" for the program. Using "people" like this means I can avoid any semblance of gender or race—more realistic figures can't help looking like a man or a woman, instantly eliminating half the audience. And in the final versions, the figures are blue, which, apart from creatures in the movie *Avatar,* is not a skin color that appears often in humans, as far as I know.

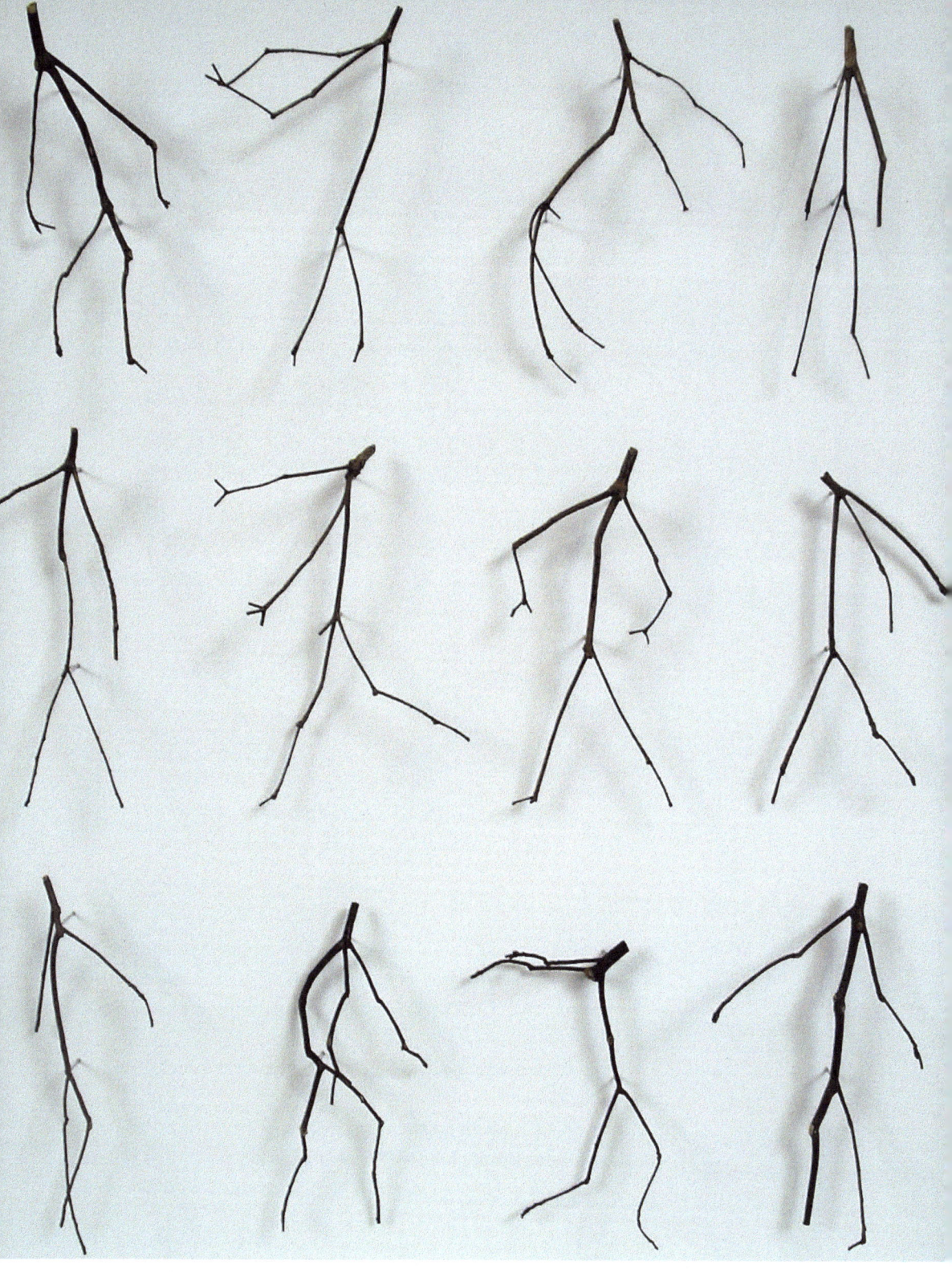

I love these *literal* stick figures by the artist Chris Kenny (↑). Elegantly twisting twigs show us how easy it is to recognize a human being (and subtle human movements), with the simplest arrangement of lines.

Twelve Twigs, 2012. See more at chriskenny.co.uk

Exercise for the tongue

In Chapter 4—with my tongue firmly in my cheek (at that time)—I mentioned tongue muscles. Actually, your tongue is *mostly* muscle. There are primarily two groups of four muscles in your mouth working to help you speak, taste, and swallow.

• Superior longitudinal lingual
• Inferior longitudinal lingual
• Transversus linguae
• Verticalis linguae

The first group (←) consists of four **intrinsic** muscles that alter the **shape** of the tongue. These muscles are not attached to any bones, and are largely inside the tongue.

The second group is four **extrinsic** muscles (↓) that alter the **position** of the tongue. These four *are* attached to bones.

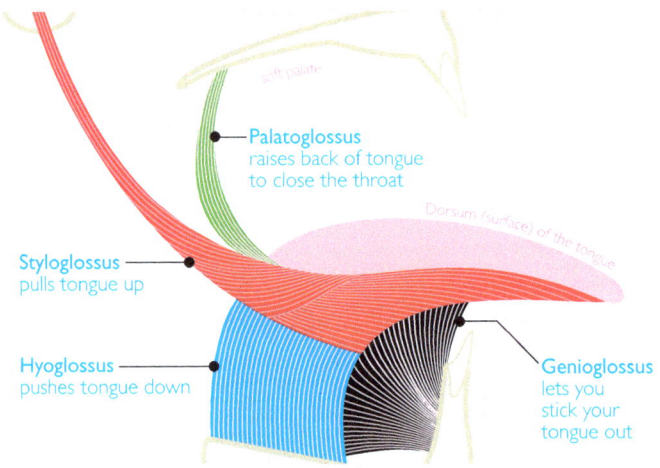

Palatoglossus
raises back of tongue to close the throat

Styloglossus
pulls tongue up

Hyoglossus
pushes tongue down

Genioglossus
lets you stick your tongue out

Three theories about the origin of **Cat got your tongue?**
1. In the 18th and 19th centuries, naughty English sailors were flogged into submission and silence with the **cat o'nine tails,** a whip with nine knotted leather straps.
2. In the Middle Ages, people equated **witches with black cats**, and they stole the tongue of anyone telling on them.
3. Ancient Egyptians worshipped cats, and when people spoke against the government or established religion, their tongues were cut out and **fed to cats**.

One way to exercise the muscles in your mouth is by reciting tongue twisters. You will stretch and strengthen the muscles, have some fun, and no cats will get your tongue (←).

Here are some tongue twisters. We all know this famous one:

She sells sea shells by the sea shore

It was originally published in 1850 as a diction exercise. The term "*tongue twister*" first appeared in 1895, and it became the lyric for a popular song in 1908.

The sixth sick sheik's sixth sheep's sick

This one is reputed to be the hardest workout for your tongue (in the English language).

These two examples mostly exploit the sound of the letter **S** being easily mistaken—or mis-spoken—for **TH**, which a common phoneme error. (Another is mis-speaking **L** for **R**.) It's all about where your tongue is in relation to your teeth when you try to say the words.

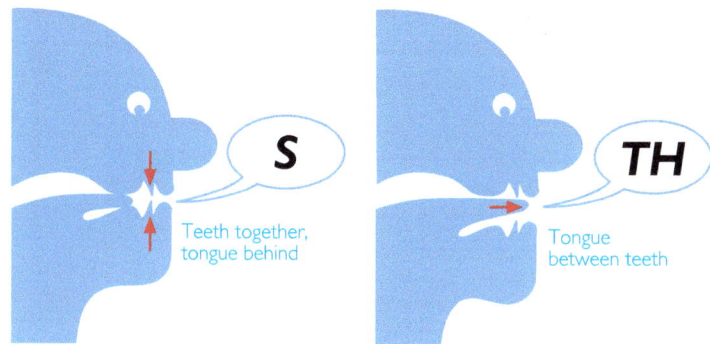

Teeth together, tongue behind

Tongue between teeth

Some more **S-TH** ones to add to your exercise routine:
So this is the sushi chef

The seething sea ceaseth,
and thus the seething sea sufficeth us

Selfish shellfish

There's an official Tongue Twister Day (along with almost anything you can name*). It's the second Sunday in November, and it was inspired by the annual International Tongue Twister Contest, first held in 2008 at the Logic Puzzle Museum in Burlington, Wisconsin.

*For instance:
Dance Like a Chicken Day?
That's May 14th
National Prune Day?
It's June 15th
(from nationaltoday.com)

Nick Stoeberl, of Salinas, California, probably takes longer doing tongue exercises than most of us do: The *Guinness Book of Records* says that he has the longest tongue in the world (↓). It is huge.

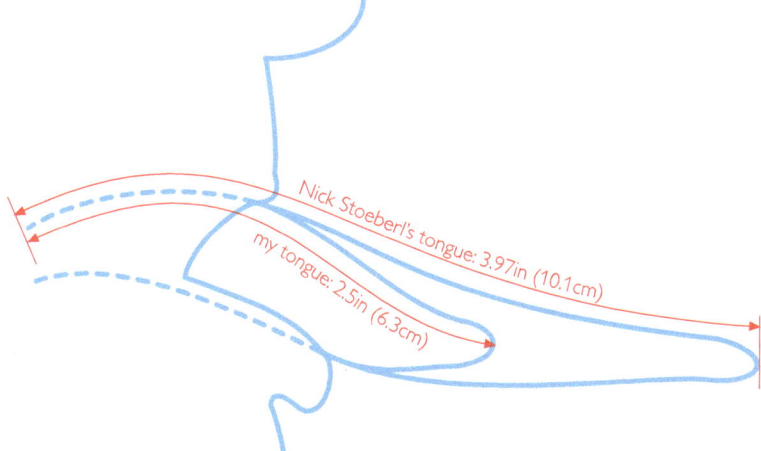

Nick Stoeberl's tongue: 3.97in (10.1cm)

my tongue: 2.5in (6.3cm)

Confusion abounds about how to measure the length of a tongue. If you look at a photo of Nick sticking his tongue out, it doesn't appear to be nearly four inches long from his top lip to the tip of the tongue—which is how *Guinness* says measurements should be made. In my version (←), I go to the back of the mouth, where the tongue starts.

OK, leth twist and get our tungth fit!
(After all, this *is* a book about exercise.)

Just sitting around

Robert Silk is hoping that an idea of his—competitive chair-sitting—will become a recognized sport. It's an endurance activity that involves sitting for long periods of time in unfriendly environments (weather-wise), with no digital devices, just doing nothing. In 2020, he sat in Joshua Tree National Park, in California, for 14 hours and 27 minutes. He's also done a spell of sitting in Antarctica. Silk's is not the first endurance-sitting idea. In the Netherlands, Pole Sitting (*paalzitten* →) is a "sport" where competitors sit on top of wooden poles for hours to see who can stay there the longest.

Since the title of this last chapter is *et cetera*—meaning "and the rest"—I'll finish with something that I've mentioned before: the importance of REST. OK, I do know the original Latin phrase meant "rest" in a different sense—please forgive my silly play on a word. But silliness is almost the point, because I would add something to REST that to me is equally important: F U N.

"And fun" in Latin would be *et delicia*—isn't that nice!

Look at these great turns of phrase about resting from Spain and Italy, and one from France about the importance of folly, a word that makes me think not so much of madness, as delight in unnecessary things, like *follies*—decorative but useless little buildings in grand old English country house gardens, where the architects were just having some fun.

Doing nothing, resting, having fun; these are all elements of staying fit. Earlier in the book, I mentioned why it's good to let your body rest in between workouts—even to take a day off—rather than pushing on all the time. But what about having fun *while* you are exercising?

There's a place where you can do just that: *Clown Cardio.* Jaymie Parkkinen started it in Los Angeles in 2023. (He points out that no one wears garish makeup.) In the one-hour *Clown Cardio* class, participants are encouraged to be silly, indeed Jaymie measures the success of his exercises—which are more like games, with loud music—by the amount of laughter generated.

theclowncardio.com

While laughter may not build your muscles, it does boost the release of endorphins, giving you what runners experience when they get a "runners' high."

I'm all for having a good time while exercising, but I do think *Clown Cardio* is an odd choice of name. Many people are afraid of clowns or find them creepy, and so as a designer—if I was asked for my opinion!—I'd suggest *Comedy Cardio* (or *Cardio Comedy*) might be a better name. But I would give a nasal nod to clowns with a relaxed, casual logo.

Fear of clowns is called *coulrophobia*, a term that was first used in the 1980s.

For scary/creepy, think *Pennywise* from Stephen King's *It*, or John Wayne Gacy as *Pogo* (or even *Ronald McDonald*).

If you need any proof of what fun can do when it comes to our well-being, consider these funny people whose healthy sense of humor has made us laugh over the years, and kept them going:

Al Jaffee (*Mad* magazine cartoonist), 102
Norman Lear, 101
George Burns, 100
Bob Hope, 100
Mel Brooks, 99
Dick Van Dyke, 99 (→)
Carl Reiner, 98
Phyllis Diller, 95

I don't know about his exercise routine (although he is a great dancer), but Dick Van Dyke is quoted as saying that he has been lucky to be able to "play and act silly" for a living.

THE END

Thank you

First, to Elliott Morsia in London and Alberto Cairo in Florida who shepherded this, my second book with them for CRC Press, with a lot of friendly help and a whole lot of patience. My eternal thanks.

A big thank you to my three experts, Dr. Phillip Kasofsky (Dr. K), Gene deNota, and Marion Nestle, who generously gave me the time and help I needed to make sure what I wrote was 'fit' to print.

(Since that was a slightly childish reference to *The New York Times'* front page mantra (→), I should say that one glance at my list of articles consulted will show you that I have found *NYT*'s reporting in the health and fitness area to be an invaluable source of inspiration. Thank you to all the great writers there.)

"All the News
That's Fit to Print"

Samar Haddad was an extremely attentive copyreader, saving me from many embarrassing typos and inconsistencies. I feel lucky to have had her sharp eyes (and general sensibility) by my side.

Thank you to my fellow information designers in Chapter 8—Álvaro Valiño, Andy Kirk, Heather Jones, Jason Forrest, John Grimwade, Kenneth Field, Luigi Farrauto, Ole Munk, Paul Mijksenaar, Renée Klein, RJ Andrews, and Steve Duenes—for letting me know what they do for exercise, and for taking the time to make it graphic. And to Bonnie Berkowitz and Laura Stanton, whose piece about their colleagues' office workouts first appeared in *The Washington Post.*

Thank you to Ben Keyser for informing me about the difference between tennis elbow and golfer's elbow; to Jan Martin and Nancy Pierson for telling me about their energetic tennis routines; to Peter and Shelley Dobyns, and Hauke Kite-Powell for describing their exhausting experience in the Paris-Brest-Paris cycle event.

Thank you to Eric Gill for drawing the typeface you are reading here. Gill is a controversial figure for reasons that have nothing to do with design, but his 1927 font (Gill Sans) is great. (So there.)

Thank you as ever, Rowland, for making sure my computer does what *I* want it to do, and for selflessly producing a wonderful website for the book.

Thank you to my darling wife Erin. As a non-designer, you are the perfect person to read my drafts, and pose "what do you mean by this?" questions, without ever mentioning that I might be spending too much time in the "office." Forever, sweetheart.

Articles/links consulted (Upper and lower case here is as it appeared in the respective headlines)

A Conversation with Marion Nestle, Mary Duenwald, *New York Times*, 2/19/2002

A Quixotic Quest For Longevity Adds a Sales Pitch, Christopher Beam, *New York Times*, 1/14/2024

All About Ozempic and the Next Generation of Obesity Drugs, Dani Blum, *New York Times*, 5/20/2024

At 93, he's as fit as a 40-year-old, Gretchen Reynolds, *Washington Post*, 1/16/2024

At 95, World's Oldest Speedskater Has Given Up on Retiring, Martin Fackler and Hisako Ueno, *New York Times*, 3/23/2025

Behind the push for padel, Christopher Cameron, *Washington Post*, 1/9/2024

Best Measure of Health? Body Roundness Index Finds Support over B.M.I., Roni Caryn Rabin, *New York Times*, 2024

Broccoli: All They Say It Is, Caroline Hopkins Legaspi, *New York Times*, 10/22/2024

Brown Fat, C. Clairborne Ray, *New York Times*, 3/12/2002

Can Weed Improve a Workout? Hilary Achauer, *New York Times,*, 3/26/2024

Chronic Exercise Preserves Lean Muscle Mass in Masters Athletes, Andrew P. Wroblewski et al., *The Physician and Sportsmedicine*, September, 2011

Clown Cardio Doesn't Take Exercise Too Seriously, Lucky Benson, *New York Times*, 1/21/2024

Come on lads, stretch yourselves, Matt Munday, *London Sunday Times Magazine*, 2023

Could exercise pills help create a healthier society? David Cox, *The Guardian*, 12/31/2023

Could You Pass the Presidential Physical Fitness Test Today? Danielle Friedman, *New York Times*, 2/20/2024

David Sedaris, Dressed Up With Nowhere to Go, Sarah Lyall, *New York Times*, 6/20/2020

Dick Van Dyke, Approaching 99, Dances in Coldplay's Latest Video, Derrick Bryson Taylor, *New York Times*, 12/9/2024

Dietary Fats Explained, pubmed.ncbl.nlm.nih.gov/24239922/

Difficult Exercises Deserve a Little Love, Anna Maltby, *New York Times*, 3/6/2024

Elaine LaLanne, a Grande Dame of Fitness, Danielle Friedman, *New York Times*, 10/3/2023

Evangelist for Longevity Urges Fasting,, Jason Horowitz, *New York Times*, 3/28/2024

Even Celebrities Don't know How to Ask Their Friends About Ozempic, Callie Holtermann and Danu Blum, *New York Times*, 4/30/2024

Every step above 2,200 steps a day reduces risk of early death, Tobi Thomas, *The Guardian*, 3/6/2024

Exercise May Lead to Better Sleep, Hannah Singleton, *New York Times*, 12/3/2024

Exercise to Strengthen Your Bones, Danielle Friedman, *New York Times*, 6/11/2024

Fat factors, Robin Marantz Henig, *New York Times Magazine*, 8/13/2006

Fitness Myths You Need to Stop Falling For, Danielle Friedman, *New York Times*, 1/9/2024

Five Exercises to keep an Aging Body Strong and Fit, Connie Chang, *New York Times,*, 3/1/2023

Five Health Benefits of Belly Dance, Zarafshan Shiraz, *Hindustan Times*, 1/13/2021

For a Stable, Strong Core, Forget About Crunches, Jenny Marder, *New York Times,*, 2/8/2023

Fox Hunter's New Tack, Amelia Nierenberg, *New York Times*, 8/27/2024

GPS Watch? No Way. Some Elite Runners Are Ditching the Data, Scott Cacciola, *New York Times*, 9/16/2023

'Health Halo,' Dani Blum, *New York Times*, 10/20/2024

High-Intensity Training, But Dialed Back a Bit, Jen Murphy, *New York Times*, 5/28/2024

Hitting the Wall, Wikipedia, 6/2/2024

How Bad are Ultraprocessed Foods, Really? Alice Callahan, *New York Times*, 5/6/2024

How do dimples in golf balls affect their flight? Tom Veilleux, *Scientific American*, 8/19/2005

How Exercise Strengthens Your Brain, Dana G. Smith, *New York Times*, 4/2/2024

How Important Is Stretching, Really? Hannah Seo, *New York Times*, 12/15/2022

How Long Does It Take to Get Fit Again? Knvul Sheik, *New York Times*, 1/30/2024

How to Buy Yourself a Longer Life, Frank Bruni, *New York Times*, 5/23/2024

How to Get the Most Out of a Treadmill Desk, Amanda Loudin, *New York Times*, 5/2/2024

How to live forever; the science of immortality, Ryan Yling, *The Greyhound*, 2024

How to Make Squats Easier on Your Knees, Adele Jackson-Gibson, *New York Times*, 9/17/2024

How to Shop Like a Nutrition Scientist, Jancee Dunn, *New York Times*, 1/14/2025

How to Spare Yourself From Shoulder Pain, Cindy Kuzma, *New York Times*, 12/29/2022

In the Age of Ozempic, She's Fighting for the Freedom to Be Fat, Lisa Miller, *New York Times*, 14/22/2024

Is Heat Actually Good for Sore Muscles? Emma Yasinski, *New York Times*, 5/30/2024

Is The Secret to a Longer Life Hidden in a Transplant Drug? Dana G. Smith, *New York Times*, 9/25/2024

Keep fit and keep your figure, Eileen Fowler, *Radio Times*, 1/31/1958

Leonard Hayflick, Who Discovered Why No One Lives Forever, Clay Risen, *New York Times*, 8/17/2024

Living and Dying in 3/4 Time, Maureen Dowd, *New York Times*, 8/10/2023

Making A Racket: Millions of Americans Now Play Pickleball, Chartr, 2024

Men and other mammals live longer if they are castrated says researcher, Ella Creamer, *The Guardian (USA)*, 6/1/2014

Meet the Man Who Wants to Make Sitting an Extreme Sport, Laura Kiniry, *New York Times*, 4/12/2022

Muscles in Knots? Danielle Friedman, *New York Times*, 5/14/2024

New Weight Loss Drugs Make Cear That Body Size Is Not a Choice, Julia Belluz, *New York Times*, 2/2/2023

1970s Hit Resonates as Paean To a Drug, Craig Marks, *New York Times*, 2024

Oprah Ozempic and US, Tressie McMillan Cottom, *New York Times*, 3/24/2024

Patients Hate 'Forever' Drugs. Is Wegovy Different? Gina Kolata, *New York Times*, 3/24/2024

Paying Greater Attention to One's 'Health Span,' Dana G. Smith, *New York Times*, 12/3/2024

Performance-Enhanced Games, Calum Marsh, *New York Times*, 11/24/2024

Relax With the Confidence of Knowing You're No Slouch, Matt Richtel, *New York Times*, 4/30/2024

Review of 'Food Politics,' Marion Nestle, *The Economist*, 5/11/2002

Routine Is a Foe in Strength Training, Hilary Achauer, *New York Times*, 5/14/2024

Stepping Out, David Sedaris, *The New Yorker*, 6/30/2014

Study of Life Spans Suggests Humans May Be at Their Peak, Dana G. Smith, *New York Times*, 2024

Supershoes are reshaping distance running, Jonathan W. Rosen, *MIT Technology Review*, 6/25/2024

Supplement Stores Are Trying to Tap Into the Ozempic Boom, Jordyn Holman, *New York Times*, 5/2/2024

Sweet and Vicious, the case against sugar, Gary Taubes, *New York Times Magazine*, 4/17/2011

The Fitness Information in Your Heart Rate, Talya Minsberg, *New York Times*, 3/27/2023

The History of Fitness, Lance Dalleck, *IDEA Health and Fitness Association*, 1/10/2011

The History of Physical Fitness, Erwan Le Corre, artofmanliness.com, 10/1/23

The man who couldn't stop eating, Atul Gawande, *The New Yorker*, 7/9/2001

The Obesity Warriors, Claudia Wallis, Special Issue of *Time* Magazine, 6/7/2004

The quest to legitimize longevity medicine, Jessica Hamzelou, *MIT Technology Review*, 3/18/2024

Three Ways to Measure How Fit You Are, Dana G. Smith, *New York Times*, 3/27/2023

Three Ways to Test Yourself, Hilary Achauer, *New York Times*, 7/2/2024

Trials Show that Obesity Drug may Relieve Arthritis Pain, Gina Kolata, *New York Times*, 11/2/2024

Ultraprocessed Foods, Carlos Monteiro et al., *Public Health Nutrition*, 2/12/2019

Welcome to the AI gym staffed by virtual trainers, Rhiannon Williams, *MIT Technology Review*, 10/9/2022

What is the Keto Diet and Does it Work? Dawn MacKeen, *New York Times*, 1/2/2020

What Muscles Does a Bike Work? Onepeloton.com/blog/, accessed 2/19/24

What Popular Fitness Fads Get Wrong, Talya Minsberg, *New York Times*, 3/21/2024

When Is the Best Time to Work Out? Alexander Nazarayan, *New York Times*, 5/4/2024

Why Do We Age? Dana G. Smith, *New York Times*, 3/25/2024

Why Do We Call Them 'Dumbbells'? Jake Rossen, Mentalfloss.com, 6/7/2025

Why Ultraprocessed Foods Are So Irresistible, Alice Callahan, *New York Times*, 8/1/2024

Why You Don't Need to Exercise Every Day, Calum Marsh, *New York Times,* 7/15/2024
Would Getting a Pet Help You Live Longer? Lybi Ma, *Psychology Today,* 2/13/2024

Books and Magazines consulted

AMA Encyclopedia of Medicine, Charles Clayman, Editor, Random House, 1989
Overcoming Obesity in America, Special Issue of *Time* Magazine, 6/7/2004
Physical Fitness, Penguin Books, 1965
PowerGolf, Ben Hogan, Gallery Books, 1948
Return to Life through Contrology, William Miller, 1960
Rules of the Game, The Diagram Group, Bantam Books, 1976
Sports Comparisons, The Diagram Group, Arthur Barker Limited, 1982
Stretching, Bob Anderson, Shelter Publications, 1982
The Book of Comparisons, The Diagram Group, Penguin Books, 1980
The Human Body, Charles Clayman, Editor, DK Publishing, 1995
The Natural Method (3 volumes), Georges Hébert, 1909, translated by Philippe Til
The Science of Exercise, Time Magazine Special Edition, Dotdash Meredith, 2023
The Story of Hanoverian and Modern Britain, C.W.Airne, Sankey Hudson & Co., c. 1930
The World's Best Anatomical Charts, Springhouse Corporation, 2000
Time Atlas of the Body, Rand McNally, 1976
Ultimate Training Guide, Men's Health Magazine, Richard Dorment, editor, 2024
Ultimate Workout Guide, Women's Health Magazine, Liz Plosser, editor, 2024
Yoga Anatomy, Leslie Kaminoff & Amy Matthews, Human Kinetics, 2007
Yoga, 101 Essential Tips, Lucinda Hawksley & Ian Whitelaw, editors, DK Publishing, 1995

Credits